Creating Autoethnographies

Creating Autoethnographies

Tessa Muncey

SAGE

Los Angeles | London | New Delhi
Singapore | Washington DC

4772285950

SAGE Publications Ltd
1 Oliver's Yard
55 City Road
London EC1Y 1SP

SAGE Publications Inc.
2455 Teller Road
Thousand Oaks, California 91320

SAGE Publications India Pvt Ltd
B 1/I 1 Mohan Cooperative Industrial Area
Mathura Road
New Delhi 110 044

SAGE Publications Asia-Pacific Pte Ltd
33 Pekin Street #02-01
Far East Square
Singapore 048763

Library of Congress Control Number available

British Library Cataloguing in Publication data

A catalogue record for this book is available from the British Library

ISBN 978-1-84787-472-6
ISBN 978-1-84787-473-3 (pbk)

Typeset by Glyph International, Bangalore, India
Printed in India at Replika Press Pvt Ltd
Printed on paper from sustainable resources

TABLE OF CONTENTS

ACKNOWLEDGEMENTS

I am indebted to far too many individuals to mention, who have provided guidance, support, role modelling and food for thought throughout my life. However, this text would be the poorer but for the generous support and contributions from Jeni Boyd, David Carless, Kitrina Douglas, Aimee Ebersold, Amy Pinney and Sarah Wall.

PERMISSIONS

The Thirteenth Tale by Diane Setterfield (Orion Books, an imprint of The Orion Publishing Group, London, 2006)

From Paddy Clark Ha Ha Ha by Roddy Doyle, published by Secker and Warburg. Reprinted by permission of The Random House Group Ltd

PREFACE

The challenge of mutual understanding among people is arguably one of the greatest dilemmas of the 21st century. Lack of shared understanding permeates political, cultural, artistic and scientific practices and leads us into war, unrealistic healthcare practice, misunderstood groups of excluded people and much more besides. One aim of research is to find general explanations for defining people's behaviour. By rigorously defining the sample in each study, attempts are made to understand populations and through this the individuals who make up the populations. Attempts are made to identify why people may be excluded from research studies, but these are not always well documented. Those eliminated may be people whose complexity would contribute so many intervening variables that they would distract the purpose of the study and are therefore gently cast aside.

It is the complexity of individuals that autoethnography seeks to address; the muddled, idiosyncratic, florid eccentricities that make us unique as opposed to part of a population. The unexamined assumptions that govern everyday life, behaviour and decision making are as strong as any overt beliefs. The shape and size of these unexamined assumptions can be considered the staple diet of the autoethnographer. If we consider that the dominant voice of the research world is not representing our experience, then we have to find ways of redressing the balance. One only has to consider the whole discourse about adherence to medical regimens and the inherent problems in getting individuals to comply with professional advice to know that something happens when individuals interpret that advice using their own specific set of assumptions, or when the individual's set of assumptions overrides the opinion of an expert.

In order to contribute to or subvert the dominant discourses that underpin much of our research, strategies and techniques need to be found for portraying experiences that don't rely on the affinity of shared assumptions. This text sets out to unpick some of the assumptions implicit in the autoethnographer's mind, as they craft an autoethnography, identify and address some of the tensions and criticisms that the concept attracts and provide some criteria for assessing the credibility of the autoethnographic contribution. Published work has a tendency to focus on the successful: the rags to riches, victim to survivor, stories of successful research outcomes, and shies away from those with mistakes or of which we are ashamed.

I believe there are at least two reasons for reading or browsing through this book while engaging in either learning about, or engaging in, the research process. First there may be those who want to include a personal story in their study or paper and want to find a theoretical justification to do so to keep some publisher or supervisor happy. Second, there may be those who have a hint of a story to tell and want some ideas about how to set about it creatively. Of course, the two are not mutually exclusive but they represent two important assumptions of the research process: the necessity to position the work in a recognisable theoretical framework; and to present that work in a way that is congruent with the text. Of course, herein lie two assumptions that you can tease out of my thinking: first, that I don't intend to encourage anarchy in the research process; and second, that the work being created is intended for academic recognition or publishing rather than personal amusement.

EMERGING TRENDS

There are several emerging trends in qualitative research within the humanities and social sciences that correspond with the expansion of autoethnographic texts. One is the growing acceptance of the individual in research, albeit often described as deviant cases. Potter (1996, p. 138) uses the term 'deviant case' to highlight 'exactly the kind of problem that shows why the standard pattern should take the form that it does'. Typically this is research wherein an individual is identified who doesn't appear to fit within the researcher's emergent themes and is singled out for detailed scrutiny. This occurred in my own research when one student nurse appeared to contradict the pattern that was emerging from the rest of her cohorts in the study (Muncey, 2000). I believe it also happens when individuals exhibit such behaviour as child murder; behaviour that we find so abhorrent that we don't want to accept it as part of a continuum of human actions, but as some 'evil' or inhuman one-off act that we can contain as a deviancy. A good example of attempting to better understand the continuum from an individual perspective, without trying to excuse the crime, is illustrated in *Cries Unheard: The story of Mary Bell* (Sereny, 1998). Sereny suggests that the circumstances wherein a child becomes a killer cannot be divorced from an understanding of her terribly damaged life.

Second, there is the therapeutic or emancipatory element associated with participating in research. In order to reconstruct a narrative or 'lived experience', the researcher provides the participant with a cathartic experience during the collecting of the data. This is exemplified by Arthur Frank (1997, p. xii) who suggests that 'seriously ill people are wounded not just in body but in voice. They need to become storytellers in order to recover the voices that illness and its treatments often take away'.

Third, there is a growing trend for the authority of the recipients or end users of research to have a voice within the research process, and narratives have become a common source of evaluative material. This is epitomised by the powerful impact of a mother's story of the effect of antipsychotic drugs on her son, which highlighted the dispute with psychiatric opinion (Bray et al., 2008).

Autoethnography attempts to unite these trends in imaginative and insightful ways. However, because the author and the subject are the same, most published work – which can be text, performance, poetry, songs or art – is the 'story' itself, rather than an account of how it can be produced. There is a growing appeal for researchers in the disciplines of humanities and social sciences to work together, and this book should appeal to you if you are interested in using creative methods in research and come from disciplines, such as healthcare, education, communications and sport sciences, that draw on the social sciences.

SHAPE AND FORM OF THE BOOK

The shape of the book will mirror the process of writing about experience, from the establishment of an idea, through the process of writing, the development of skills to enhance the text, to worked examples of the whole process. At the same time, an indication of resources that can be drawn on to counter some of the criticisms and tensions within the field will be provided.

The form of the book will be to engage in the narrative devices of 'showing' and 'telling'. 'Telling' is the device for exploring the issues as they have been described in the various literatures that underpin the approach; and 'showing' is using examples of autoethnographic text not only to provide illustration, but also to allow you, the reader, to engage in your own imaginative relationship to the text.

Summaries will be provided to highlight key points as you work through the process of creating your own autoethnography.

THE JOURNEY THROUGH THE BOOK

Researchers ask questions and attempt to find answers and autoethnographers are no exception. Why do autoethnography? Where does my own experience fit the existing literature? What does my experience add to existing ideas and what new slant could I bring to an established body of knowledge? **Chapter 1** sets out to examine some of these questions. Towards the end of a research study that made up my PhD, I realised that I was more interested in one individual than in the group I had set out to investigate. This chapter will describe the awakening and discovery of my own story and extrapolate the issues from this that I think underpin the rationale for using autoethnography.

A key component of the background to an autoethnographic account is the composition of the personal world from which the account derives. **Chapter 2** will outline the characteristics of personal worlds that provide a framework for engaging in and ultimately reviewing others' autoethnographies. This will set the scene for the highly contentious issue of what is meant by the concept of self, which will be returned to in Chapter 4 when dealing with issues of legitimacy.

Justification for a particular approach is an important part of the research process, particularly when the sample involves very small numbers of people. **Chapter 3** will provide an overview of the ways in which individual stories have been utilised in research and consider the origins of, and current debates within, autoethnography. While not providing an exhaustive account, some consideration will be given to alternative approaches such as narrative and phenomenology, in order to provide a practical and philosophical justification for portrayal of individual experience as an important contribution to research.

The layers of a person's experience that are revealed in an autoethnography can often expose a very vulnerable self that requires thoughtful writing tactics. This involves techniques for releasing creativity and stimulating the imagination. **Chapter 4** will address the planning of an account and introduce practical hints to enhance the creative process. These will include the use of the snapshot to describe both literary and pictorial episodes. The stimulus of artefacts will be introduced to conjure up feelings and thoughts, and the uses of metaphor to enable deeply personal experiences to be layered and disguised without losing meaning. Ethical considerations play a part in this because most stories involve other people.

Publication of autoethnographic texts elicits a variety of concerns within the wider academic community. Foremost in these concerns is to what extent the experience can be extrapolated for others and how a retort of self indulgence can be avoided. **Chapter 5** sets out to address the legitimacy of autoethnography and to confront one of the most challenging voices of disapproval, that of autoethnography being superficial, self-indulgent navel gazing. This text may not provide enough evidence to convince the ardent holder of this view but it should provide enough ammunition to defend the approach within a broadly sympathetic audience. Starting with a consideration of the self in research and the implications of this for telling one's own story, I will use the reactions to telling my own story to tease out some of these concerns. The analysis and interpretation of autoethnographic texts requires the reader to utilise a broader range of analytical skills than those used for other research methods – skills more associated with the humanities, such as linguistic, semantic and aesthetic analysis, and literary criticism. This chapter will also consider the parts that truth and resonance play in understanding the autoethnographic text, and consider the role of memory in recalling those experiences.

Using biographical details of people can be ethically challenging. **Chapter 6** will demonstrate how the use of a composite character whereby a typical person is constructed can overcome this difficulty. Using an autoethnographic study, *Positions of Vulnerability* (Ebersold Silva, 2004), as an illustration, this chapter will demonstrate how the composite character of Lois, a drug user, can be drawn from the author's experience and used to interweave with her own story to draw attention to the issue of counter-transference in the therapeutic relationship. A composite character is one way of avoiding the ethical issues that are an integral part of using individual's stories. This account also draws me, as supervisor of the piece of research, into the frame, and considers how the risks, responsibilities and vulnerabilities extend beyond the novice researcher to the academy.

To draw the threads of the book together, **Chapter 7** will explore the whole journey of an autoethnographic experience, culminating in the writing of a song outlining the ideas, background and creative processes, which will serve to demonstrate the similarities that exist between composing music and writing text, but also illuminate the process in a fresh way.

In the brief route map of the path through this text, I have 'told' you what you can expect to find; but before I start let me 'show' you another way of looking at the assumptions that underpin this way of communicating.

EXPERIENCING THE BOOK

Beginning a book about the process of creating autoethnographies is rather like asking a cook to write about the experience of cooking. Instead of producing perfectly formed meals for you to admire and enjoy and evaluate her prowess, the cook will have to make certain assumptions about the readership. She might check out some of the assumptions she has about the equipment in your kitchen and the skills you have in certain cooking techniques, but I suspect she won't for one minute think she needs to explain about the role of food in staying alive and healthy, or question whether you have access to a kitchen in which to follow her recipes. She will tell you when to add baking powder to a recipe, but not expect you to know the chemical formulation of how baking powder works. You will choose a recipe book that reflects your own world view about cooking – whether you want precise instructions or general hints; whether you want illustrations to show finished results or find this intimidating; whether you are a beginner or an experienced cook looking for inspiration; but no one book can answer all the questions. So as I start on this experience of writing, I am reminded to explore my own underlying assumptions about the thoughts, ideas, talents, skills, memories and hopes that I have for creating autoethnographies, some of which are influenced by what I have read, the life I have lived, the subjects I have studied, the jobs I have done and the many memorable individuals with whom I have journeyed, both physically and metaphorically.

WHO AM I?

Who am I to engage in this feat, and what writers, philosophers, literary critics, poets, artists, and authors of both fiction and academic texts should I hold up to the mirror of my own ideas? If anyone thinks that it must be easier to write only about oneself, then they have not grasped the complexity of constructing an autoethnographic text and attempting to position it within a framework which will be accepted by the audience it intends to reach. This in itself raises questions about who the audience is, the acceptable style and its academic traditions, and whether the written word is the best medium for the message.

I suspect a great many autoethnographies at least start off as oral presentations of some kind, either as part of a teaching session, as mine have, or oral conference presentations that later turn into written text. Bachelard (1994, p. xxxix) recognises the considerable task of translating ideas from 'speaking uninhibitedly to a friendly audience' to writing a book. In lecturing he suggests we may 'become animated by the joy of teaching and, at times, our words think for us … writing a book requires really serious reflection'. This parallels the experience of writing an autoethnography – taking a personal experience and casting it to the vicissitudes of a sometimes hostile academic world.

Even the process of introducing myself becomes problematic when it is to become part of a fixed text that cannot adapt and flex, dependent on my mood or the group I am with. When I talk about autoethnography in class, it is easy to spend a few minutes introducing myself. I often do this with the help of a few preselected snapshots that give a quick glimpse into the many facets of who I am at that time. 'Who am I?' must be the ultimate autoethnographic question, and I set out some responses for your contemplation.

Who am I?

I was born a girl at a time when it was politically, socially, educationally and professionally advantageous to be a boy.

I am a two-year-old dressed up for the Queen's Coronation where the subliminal seed of being a nurse may have been sown.

I am a fifteen-year-old escaping a home that failed to nourish and protect me.

I am a community nurse when all the accolades seem to be handed out to the institutional nurse.

I am a gardener who glories in the magic of growing things.

I am a patchwork quilter who enjoys the challenge of making order out of tiny fragments of material.

I am a foxglove: strong, proud, unique, the heart beat of my family growing up and under the protection of significant other people.

I am so much more than my CV but not yet all that I am capable of becoming.

This tiny attempt to portray something of who I am highlights many of the problems of writing creatively about experience. Experiences happen in a time and place, they have antecedents and consequences, they are subject to memory, they involve other people and there are certain aspects we may choose to ignore or which are buried in the unconscious. No writing occurs in a vacuum and in writing this text I am reflecting back on certain stages of my writing experience, at the same time as undergoing changes to my thinking as I write.

REFERENCES

Bachelard, G. (1994) *The Poetics of Space.* Beacon Press, Boston, MA.

Bray, J., Clarke, C., Brennan, G. and Muncey, T. (2008) Should we be 'pushing meds'? The implications of pharmacogenomics. *Journal of Psychiatric and Mental Health Nursing,* **15**(5), 357–64.

Ebersold Silva, A. (2004) *Positions of Vulnerability: An autoethonographic study.* Unpublished dissertation from University of Cambridge.

Frank, A. (1997) *The wounded storyteller: Body illness and ethics.* University of Chicago Press, Chicago, IL.

Muncey, T. (2000) Nursing Metaphors. In D. Freshwater (Ed.) *Making a Difference.* Nursing Praxis International, Nottingham, ch. 2.

Potter, J. (1996) Discourse Analysis and Constructionist Approaches: Theoretical background. In J. Richardson (Ed.) *Handbook of Qualitative Research Methods for Psychology and the Social Sciences.* BPS Books, Leicester.

Sereny, G. (1998) *Cries Unheard: The story of Mary Bell.* Macmillan, Basingstoke.

1
WHY DO AUTOETHNOGRAPHY? DISCOVERING THE INDIVIDUAL IN RESEARCH

CHAPTER PREVIEW

Which branch of research does it sit in?
Where does an autoethnography emerge from?
Influences
My influential individuals
The missing story
First attempt to tell the story
The case study (Muncey, 1998a)

As a researcher or reader, I hope you will have arrived at the beginning of this book with your own myriad of questions. You may feel that you have a plethora of experience that is being repressed in your desire to conduct 'proper' research. You may have discovered that your own experiences are already directing you to certain topics to satisfy this personal experience, or directing you to certain questions that need answers, or indeed you may be experiencing the impact of missing literature in your reading, the conspicuous absence of a world view or perspective that is continuously missed by writers in your field. Such is my vain hope of finding a narrative that portrays teenage pregnancy in a positive light. You will almost certainly be grappling with trying to write in a certain way and to jump through hoops to please the triumvirate of the academy, the publishing world and yourself.

I have lost count of the number of people who launch enthusiastically into the detail of their research interests and when asked why they are interested, admit sheepishly that they themselves have experience of the concept they are studying. When asked if they are writing themselves into the study, they are horrified that this blatant display of subjectivity will somehow infect the quality of their work. So if this is you, I ask you to consider what particular kind of filter you are employing to separate your own experience from what you are studying. It must be a very powerful one if you try to deny that the impact of your experience has no bearing on the way you conduct your own work. Isn't it healthier to acknowledge the link and purposely build it into your work, or even more interestingly, make yourself the focus of the study? Alternatively, you may be listening to the stories of your participants and finding that their voice is excluded from the dominant discourse of your particular discipline. This is the issue that autoethnography addresses, for as Hillman (1996, p. 17) says 'A single anecdote lights up the whole world of vision'.

WHICH BRANCH OF RESEARCH DOES IT SIT IN?

Autoethnography is a research approach that privileges the individual. It is an artistically constructed piece of prose, poetry, music or piece of art work that attempts to portray an individual experience in a way that evokes the imagination of the reader, viewer or listener. While I strongly support the idea that individual experiences are a legitimate source of data, I hesitate to call it a research method, as there are in fact many ways of including these experiences in the research process. In Wolcott's depiction of qualitative research as a tree, he portrays the various branches of qualitative research as strategies from which a variety of smaller branches spread out (Wolcott, 2001, p. 90). Ethnography and its subsidiary forms he locates in what he labels 'Participant Observation Strategies'.

The autoethnographer perches comfortably upon this branch. Not only is the individual a participant in the social context in which their experience takes place, but they are also an observer of their own story and its social location. While the branches of the tree are important conveyers of nutrients to the smaller twigs and leaves, an important aspect of the tree is buried underground. The life-sustaining roots that reach down into a fertile underworld might be likened to the unconscious mind that directs and checks our every move or the sustenance of everyday life that experiences, enquires and examines our every action. Wolcott reminds us that we do not necessarily need to know who planted the tree or how it evolved, but we do need to be secure in the position from which we do our viewing.

WHERE DOES AN AUTOETHNOGRAPHY EMERGE FROM?

In grappling with how to portray the process of doing an autoethnography, I kept returning to the notion that it somehow emerges out of the iterative process of doing research, while engaging in the process of living a life. I rarely come across people who set out to do autoethnography but I do rather meet many people who resort to it as a means of getting across intangible and complex feelings and experiences that somehow can't be told in conventional ways, or because the literature they are reading is not telling their story. In this journey of discovery some feel they make a breakthrough in conveying 'lived experience' when they discover Phenomenology; but even in this attempt to portray meaningful life experiences they feel compelled to 'bracket' their own experience in keeping with Husserl's (1970) advice.

In order to take the leap into creating an autoethnography one has first to recognise that there is no distinction between doing research and living a life. The person who suffers from a long-term condition cannot be separated from the researcher investigating it, who has him/herself experience of the condition. Just as a counsellor is both a therapist and a client, the autoethnographer is both the researcher and the researched.

INFLUENCES

None of us live in a disconnected world. We are surrounded by people, live at a particular point in history, have jobs and hobbies that unite us and dreams and experiences that separate us. In all of these influences on our lives none are perhaps more important than individuals – individuals who have inspired us, given birth to us, made us angry or even changed the course of our lives; among all these influences are the makings of our stories.

The uniqueness of individuals has a fascination for me, but I concur with Berger (2002, p. 176) that 'there is a huge gap between the experience of living a normal life at this moment on the planet and the public narratives being offered to give a sense to that life'. Berger claims that in this gap people may get lost and go mad, and attempt to fill the gaps with stories that mirror what is going on around them, rather than the official versions that they cannot connect with. Public narratives include the success and necessity of the family, when most people know of the difficulties and misery that family life entails, illustrated so effectively by Christopher Poulos (2008) in his autoethnography about family secrets. The public narratives about teenage pregnancy focus on moral decline, inadequate knowledge of contraception and sexual relationships, failing to mention the possible links with child abuse (Muncey, 1998c). These public narratives are often contained within research and the missing stories trapped in the 'empty space' are deemed too subjective or too self indulgent to report.

MY INFLUENTIAL INDIVIDUALS

I carried out my PhD as a mature student with more than 25 years' experience as a nurse and subsequently nurse educator. I therefore brought to the study a wealth of experience that could not be separated out from the focus of my thesis. On reflection, I could trace the influence of a great number of individuals who had impacted on my life and significantly altered my world view, from specific teachers to individual patients, from family members to key authors. I realised how my most influential ideas were invoked not by generalised studies but individual perspectives and chance acquaintances.

During a masters degree in women's studies, I had viewed my experience within nursing and psychology through the lens of my feminist leanings to examine the imagery surrounding the nurse and how it related to, predominantly 'her' psychological make up. In a small-scale study I used repertory grids from personal construct theory to examine the perceptions of a group of nurses and arrived at a conclusion that suggested a key feature of nurses' perceptions was of their 'need to be needed' (Muncey, 1994; Muncey, 1998b). This need to be needed was brought into sharp relief by the pathological needy behaviour of Beverley Allitt.

In 1994, at Grantham and Kesteven Hospital in the UK, Allitt was responsible for the deaths of four children and the serious injury of nine others. The Clothier (1994) enquiry's main findings also indicated a wide range of failings involving lax managerial procedures and inadequate consultant staffing, as well as clinical misjudgement by X-ray clinicians and pathologists.

These recommendations are even more exceptional in the light of a rider to them, that 'the foregoing recommendations are aimed at the tightening of procedures to safeguard children in hospital, but no measures can afford complete protection against a determined miscreant'.

By their own admission, Clothier states, 'even had everything been done correctly, it is unlikely that Allit would have been eliminated from the nursing profession' (Clothier, 1994, s. 2.16.7).

In his epilogue, Clothier (1994, p. 131) suggested that 'society has very little defence against the aimless malice of a deranged mind'; clear evidence that any restriction on recruitment would not avoid such incidents.

While the Clothier report concentrated on procedural and managerial processes, Nick Davies (1994), in his book *Murder on Ward Four*, portrays a girl who wove elaborate fantasies, craved attention and wanted above all to feel special. This made me reflect on whether Allitt could really be considered a deviant case, exhibiting pathological needs that were just one extreme end of a continuum of 'needing to be needed' that the majority of nurses manage to keep under control most of the time (Muncey, 1998b). What became very clear to me was that the report and its twelve recommendations were unable to answer the real concerns of nurse educators involved in interviewing young people who want to enter nursing. Insight into Allitt's behaviour may have shed light on the psychological traits detrimental to the effective nurse, but her story was dismissed as random and aimless.

This experience early in my research career, where 'official' narratives were at odds with individual stories, was a thread that was to recur throughout my working life. Of course none of the stories was told by Beverly herself. Sometime later, while talking to a group of paediatric nurses about the Clothier report, I actually met someone who had worked with Beverly. Far from the demonic creature represented in the media and government reports, she was described as slightly overweight, shy and quite inconspicuous. Not for the first time did I think that understanding her might have been more beneficial than understanding the catalogue of managerial and clinical mistakes that surrounded her.

Following the completion of my masters dissertation, I was left with many unanswered questions, not least of which was just how we select individuals with healthy psychological profiles to become good nurses. Inherent problems in these questions were that characteristics of the good nurse appeared to be missing in the literature, and psychological profiles appeared to depend on general characteristics from psychometric studies rather than individual ones. Undeterred, I embarked on the study but interest in the individual was never far away from my thoughts and took an unexpected twist as I neared the end of my thesis.

My thesis was a fairly conventional case study (Muncey, 2001). One cohort of student nurses was selected to follow through their three-year programme and, following a preparatory Repertory Grid analysis to generate characteristics of the good nurse, each of the cohort group was invited to participate in three repeated measures questionnaires. These questionnaires examined Locus of Control, Self-Esteem and Assertiveness Inventory. I soon discovered that this exercise taught me more about questionnaires and their limitations than it did about the students themselves. By the third year of the study, I realised that I wanted to find out more about each individual's story and invited the students to participate in personal interviews. This generated insight into the personal worlds of those who participated and gave a depth and breadth of understanding that was far more useful to me as a nurse educator than knowing about their questionnaire results.

For example, one sample of significant behaviour was how they dealt with death. One girl referred to the fact that none of the support agencies were able to provide guidance for her during her first experience of a dying patient, so she had to turn to her mother for help. On further questioning, she revealed that she came from a Romany family and then embarked on a fascinating description of the traditions and philosophical perspectives of this often misunderstood group. This aspect of her world permeated all her behaviour, with implications for support in practice, but usually going unnoticed as one of those underlying assumptions that rarely get explored.

One of the interviewees captured my attention because she was exhibiting characteristics that were not compatible with good nurse characteristics. She had problems with personal boundaries and demonstrated a view about nursing that was not in step with current practice. I was fascinated. This one individual gave me more insight into what psychological characteristics we might use to screen out individuals from the profession, so I asked my supervisor if I could spend the last part of my thesis looking at this one individual. As all good supervisors do, she wanted me to give a theoretical justification for doing this and off I went to find one. Potter (1996) came to my rescue with his discussion of deviant cases. 'Some of the most useful analytical phenomena are cases that appear to go against the pattern or are deviant in some way' (Potter, 1996, p. 138).

The deviant case can highlight exactly the kind of problem that shows why the standard pattern takes the form it does. At the time this seemed quite a compelling idea because it 'attempts to give credence to a view that does not fit with the mainstream view and may shed some light on the "other"' (Muncey, 2002); it also gave me the theoretical position that satisfied the needs of my supervisor.

Much later, I came to reflect on this position and, as my own missing story began to emerge, I had cause to reflect on the negativity of the word 'deviant': a pejorative term more related to abnormal and peculiar than to individual and interesting. Eventually, I came to believe that while a deviant case may be a disconfirmation of a pattern it may also be 'the plaintive voice of that silent majority of people whose individual voices are unheard' (Muncey, 2002).

THE MISSING STORY

The research training I received during my PhD was quite traditional, and inherent in this tradition was the ability to eliminate the self from the research setting, or to 'depopulate the research text' (Rolfe, 2002 p. 181). It is ironic that I was doing research in order to understand people better, yet at the same time was being taught to view these people as devoid of any subjectivity. As my interest in one individual cohort member grew, my own story started to seep into my thinking. I started to consider whether my own story was deviant because I found it was missing from the research I encountered in the literature and particularly at conferences.

Participation in conferences during the process of completing my PhD drew me to listen to papers purporting to explain, and subsequently offer solutions to, the 'problem' of teenage pregnancy. I would listen patiently to the researchers exploring the experience of teenage pregnancy with an air of confidence conveyed by the authority of the method they had utilised. This was an experience that I had encountered personally and I waited to hear a version that I could relate to. The explanations I kept hearing for teenage pregnancy typically fell into three main areas: health risk, moral decline and sexual ignorance; but I expected eventually to hear a version of my own truth, placing the experience within the paradigm of sexual abuse. I would occasionally ask questions. As someone who became pregnant at fifteen and was labelled a teenage mother, when would the label be removed? Was I still a teenage mother at 30, 40, 50? Was this experience frozen in a time from which I could never move on? Had the researcher ever considered that the girl may have been the subject of sexual abuse or indeed that pregnancy itself was an indicator of abuse?

These questions unsettled some researchers. On the whole they hadn't usually considered teenage pregnancy as a result of, or a form of, abuse, although there is evidence that as many as 75% of young women who become pregnant have been sexually abused. The label remained because usually they had never considered the experience in the context of the young women's whole life, just a moment frozen in time which they were trying to find ways of eliminating. One young anthropologist presenting a paper said that one of her subjects had talked about possible abuse by an uncle but she had warned her that it was better not to speculate about this if she wasn't sure. I suggested that the girl may have mistaken the researcher's interest in her as a person and made a decision to confide in her, which when rebuffed may have set back her further exploration of this for many years.

I became very disappointed at the lack of positive or successful stories and the realisation grew that, if I wanted to fill the void, I would have to tell my story in the hope that this 'evidence' might start to inform social policy in the way that the other research evidence was doing.

FIRST ATTEMPT TO TELL THE STORY

My attempt to redress the balance of evidence relating to teenage pregnancy was in retrospect rather naive. The editor of the text where my first attempt, reproduced below, was published suggested I should disguise my story as a case study and supplement it with a good review of existing evidence. No explanation was given for the concealment of my identity and I didn't think to challenge it.

THE CASE STUDY (MUNCEY, 1998A)

The Health Carer's Perspective

On 22 April a young woman was told that her pregnancy test was positive; she underwent a completely uneventful pregnancy which culminated in the birth of a very healthy baby boy on 14 December.

The girl was 15 years old. The midwife condemned her as a 'promiscuous young woman who failed to use contraceptives'. The social worker appointed to advise her said, 'just give him up for adoption and get on with your life'.

The father of the child was arrested but not charged with unlawful sexual intercourse.

The Grandmother's Tale

In an informal autobiography twenty-three years after this event, the girl's mother presented her with 'the grandmother's tale'. In it she had used her many talents to pass on fragments of her life. Photography, pressed flowers and calligraphy adorned a text that conjured up happy days amid the pleasures of the countryside; wild flowers, walks, cycling, all unfolding with a rosy glow of retrospection. Even the Second World War was set against the backdrop of the delights of new countryside when evacuated to a first teaching post in Worcestershire. However she reports that 'the twelve years of country plenty were followed by ten leaner ones back in town – out of our natural element perhaps so many things seemed to go wrong'.

The Girl's Story

In those ten lean years the girl was subjected to repeated incestuous sexual abuse. Her confusion increased, her self-esteem plummeted, she felt unable to tell anybody.

Nobody seemed surprised when after a very successful junior school education she started to fail at school. Sex became the currency of affection and nurturing; she glided effortlessly from sex at home to sex with others. Nobody asked the right questions that might have elicited the real problems. School blamed her for failing there. Family were content to let the early pregnancy be blamed on adolescent ignorance.

What none of them saw was the bleak and twisted world of a girl whose self-esteem was so blighted by her experiences that the idea of a baby to care for was, in a naive way, a treat to look forward to; a girl for whom sexual practice had been a reality for years, the unspeakable kind of incestuous relationship about which there is no one in whom to confide.

These first and subsequent attempts to tell my story paled into insignificance in the light of the reactions that they engendered. Disbelief, anger and denial made me realise how strongly held was the dominant discourse about teenage pregnancy, and what tactics might be needed to explore the story in different ways. I shall return to the issues that arise as a consequence of telling autoethnographic stories but, for now, will return to considering the constituent parts that make up a personal world.

Summary

- We are observers and participants of our own experiences: you cannot separate who you are from what you do.
- Understanding individuals is more than just a consideration of deviant cases, it can shed light on the silent majority of people whose individual voices are unheard.
- Subjectivity doesn't infect your work, it enhances it. Making links between your own experience and your work is healthy.
- Official stories can be at odds with individual stories, whereas core beliefs or experiences can permeate every aspect of our lives.
- Experiences are not frozen in time but grow and develop and therefore need creative devices for capturing the growth.
- Autoethnographies are characterised by artistically constructed pieces of 'text' that evoke the imagination and increase the reader's understanding.

FURTHER READING

Rolfe, G. (2002) Reflexive Research and the Therapeutic Use of Self. In D. Freshwater (Ed.) *Therapeutic Nursing*, ch. 10. Sage, London.

In this chapter Gary Rolfe explores the issues surrounding the use of self in the research process in order to repopulate research texts.

REFERENCES

Berger, J. (2002) *The Shape of a Pocket.* Bloomsbury, London.

Clothier, C. (1994) *Independent Inquiry Relating to Deaths and Injuries on the Children's Ward at Grantham and Kesteven General Hospital.* HMSO, London.

Davies, N. (1994) *Murder on Ward Four.* Chatto and Windus, London.

Hillman, J. (1996) *The Soul's Code: In search of character and calling.* Bantam Books, London.

Husserl, E. (1970) *The Idea of Phenomenology.* Martinus Nijoff, The Hague.

Muncey, T. (1994) 'The Medusa touch: Myths and images of nursing.' Unpublished Masters dissertation, Anglia Polytechnic University, Cambridge, pp. 100.

Muncey, T. (1998a) The Pregnant Adolescent: Sexually ignorant or destroyer of societies values? In M. Morrissey (Ed.) *Sexual Health: A nursing perspective,* ch. 7. Mark Allen Publishing, Salisbury.

Muncey, T. (1998b) Selection and retention of nurses. *Journal of Advanced Nursing,* **27**(2), 406–13.

Muncey, T. (1998c) 'Tale of a teenage mother.' *The Guardian,* 23 March, p. 17.

Muncey, T. (2001) 'The implications for selection and retention from an investigation of the relative importance of previous socialisation and current education of nurses.' Unpublished PhD thesis, Department of Applied Psychology Cranfield University.

Muncey, T. (2002) Individual Identity or Deviant Case. In D. Freshwater (Ed.) *Therapeutic Nursing,* ch. 9. Sage, London.

Potter, J. (1996) Discourse Analysis and Constructionist Approaches: Theoretical background. In J. Richardson (Ed.) *Handbook of Qualitative Research Methods for Psychology and the Social Sciences.* BPS Books, Leicester.

Poulos, C.N. (2008) Narrative conscience and the autoethnographic adventure: Probing memories, secrets, shadows, and possibilities. *Qualitative Inquiry,* **14**, 46–66.

Rolfe, G. (2002) Reflexive Research and the Therapeutic Use of Self. In D. Freshwater (Ed.) *Therapeutic Nursing,* ch. 10. Sage, London.

Wolcott, H.F. (2001) *Writing up Qualitative Research* (2nd edn). Sage, Thousand Oaks, CA.

2
PERSONAL WORLDS:
Discovering the Constituent Parts of the Individual

CHAPTER PREVIEW

Sense of self
Personal worlds
Specific consciousness and multiple worlds
Time and space
Embodiment
Emotions
Physical environment
Social context
Sense of self and agency
Values and search for meaning
Reflexiveness
A fragment of my personal world
Mixing art and science: A bridge over troubled
    waters or a bridge too far
The journey
A bridge too far?

As an autoethnographer, your story will emerge out of the juxtaposition of your own experience and outside influences, and the interaction between the two. The desire to engage in an autoethnography derives from the disjunctions that occur between one's own experience and the official narratives set out to explain it. Can you really filter out your own experience, even if you wanted to? Individuals have played an enormous part in my journey but you may find other recurring themes in your own.

Our personal worlds are complex and unique but share certain characteristics and this enables us to participate imaginatively in another person's world.

SENSE OF SELF

To most of us, our self image is a combination of whom we see in the mirror and the interaction of our physical, social, psychological and emotional sense of wellbeing in respect of that image. We are heavily influenced by the dominant voices from 19th and 20th century psychology, such as those of Freud, Skinner and Piaget, to name just a few of the founding fathers, but any encounter with the theoretical development of what is meant by self gives rise to the difficulties that can be encountered in any story about the self. This may be because there is a transient and illusive element to the self, which gives rise to doubt about the 'truth' of any stories that evolve. Romanyshyn (1982, p. 10) said that 'stories about oneself are episodic, tiny fragments taken from the continuous flow, over laid with emotion and half buried in stages of consciousness making reality an indefinable concept'.

He suggests that psychological life, his term for subjective experience, has a metaphorical character. He says the reflection in the mirror is not 'a visual double of the empirical me standing here on this side of the mirror ... when I look in the mirror I never see merely the double of myself but rather a figure in a story' (Romanyshyn 1982, p. 10).

The figure in our story can be construed as the culmination of, and glimpse into, all of the fleeting traces of our experience, mirrored in our consciousness. As Polkinghorne (1998, p. 1) reminds us, making meaning is not static, it cannot be measured, but 'it is meaningful, and human behaviour is generated and informed by this meaningfulness'.

In order to understand individuals, it seems important to think about how they see themselves, what impression these particular reflections leave. Our particular sense of self comes from a combination of our biological flow, our social context, our bodily awareness and our specific consciousness. We are aware that an important part of the self is a private, inner world of thoughts, feelings and fantasies which we only share if we choose to. We recognise a continuity from our younger selves but there is also a sense that we are continually renewed. Because of our capacity for reflexivity, we recognise the self of our experience and the self as others see us. William James first drew attention to the idea that our sense of who we are is intimately bound up with our awareness of our body and our thoughts and feelings. In his seminal text *The Principles of Psychology* (James, 1890) James's persistent concern with relations among conscious elements led him to the puzzling psychological question of the self. He argued that in every person's stream of consciousness there is a dichotomy between the 'me' and the 'not-me'. James divided the self into the 'I', the knower; and 'me', the known. However, one of the most influential theories of self was developed by Mead (1934), drawing on both James's (1890) distinction of 'I' (self as knower) and 'me' (self as known), and Cooley's (1902) theory of the looking-glass self. Cooley maintains that the self is reflected in the reactions of other people, who are the 'looking glass' for oneself. In order to understand what we are like, we need to see how others see us.

Mead also believed that knowledge of self and others develops simultaneously, both being dependent on social interaction; self and society represent a common whole and neither can exist without the other. According to Mead, this sense of self transforms our relation to the world and gives us a unique character. In being an object to ourselves we can perceive ourselves, interact with ourselves, communicate with ourselves; this self interaction can exert influence on the world in general and other people in particular. The self then is a process not a structure; the reflexive process allows us to act upon and respond to ourselves, and an important feature of this interaction is language.

PERSONAL WORLDS

Another way to perceive the world of the self is by consideration of the constituent parts of a personal world. No account of an experience can be considered without recourse to some consideration of the personal world of the individual who has constructed it. There are certain characteristics of personal worlds that might be useful to consider as you read autoethnographies or create your own. These common features provide a framework within which it is possible to consider the different levels of connection with the stories.

I am using the term personal world to mean: subjective awareness of oneself as a person and the overall pattern of personal life experiences. These experiences need to be considered in relation to aspects of self, world, experience of self and world, and the ways in which we organise experience and actions.

SPECIFIC CONSCIOUSNESS AND MULTIPLE WORLDS

The most common way to think about and write about the self has been the ego theory presenting it as a persistent entity (Blackmore, 2001). The ego theory of self emphasises the idea of unity and continuity of experience. However, Blackmore (2001, p. 525) points out that 'this apparent unity is just a collection of ever changing experiences tied together by such relationships as a physical body and a memory' and is more in keeping with bundle theory as described by Gallagher and Shear (1999). The sense of self cannot be separated from questions about consciousness, making any simple unified explanation difficult.

Jaynes (1979) suggests that consciousness is a metaphorical representation, not a direct copy of the world as experienced, and therefore any personal world is experienced from a specific viewpoint. Romanyshyn (1982) extends this idea to include the idea that consciousness is not experienced inside our heads, rather it is constituted by reflections of thoughts and feelings through the things and people outside who make up our world.

The variety of situations and people we encounter can lead us to feel that we inhabit multiple worlds. The self may appear to be a unifying feature but, depending on the context, we can exhibit and/or experience a different form of our personal world.

TIME AND SPACE

Within our conscious awareness there is a sense of the movement of time. Any narrative will represent a flow of experiences, actions and events. Pervading any present experience is an implicit awareness of events which have happened before and which may happen in the future. Our current world view may be seen to be a distillation of life so far, coloured by an anticipation of what life may hold in the future. Coupled with a sense of time is a sense of space. Our experiences are located in specific settings with differing qualities. Settings such as home may have a special emotional significance compared to work.

EMBODIMENT

Our personal worlds are inextricably coupled with a physical body, which makes our experiences seem vulnerable and transient as we gradually become conscious that our existence is limited. Biological functioning can be a constraint but the body can also be a means of expression. 'The human being is an embodied social agent' (Nettleton and Watson, 1998, p. 9), and this sense of embodiment is central to the ideas of Merleau-Ponty (1962), who proposes that all human perception is embodied, and that our senses cannot function independently of our bodies.

Shilling (1993, p. 5) talks of the human body as a project, an entity in the process of 'becoming' and Foucault (1988) has written of the 'practices' or 'technologies' of the self, the ways in which individuals internalise modes and rules of behaviour, emotion and thought and apply them in everyday life. This goes some way to explain why individuals voluntarily adopt practices and representations and why they become emotionally committed to taking certain positions in discourses. Grosz (1990, p. 65) suggests that these practices 'inscribe' or 'write' upon the body, marking it in culturally specific ways which are then 'read' or interpreted by others. Nowhere is this more evident than around the area of body image, food and eating. Lupton (1996, p. 17) describes the importance of physical appearance in western society and the extent to which control over one's body is 'a potent symbol of the extent to which their "owners" possess self control'.

The discourse around physical violence and resulting trauma draws attention to the embodiment of memories, where the experience is suppressed and subsequently 'finds it repressed by some part of himself which functions as a stranger, hiding self from the self's experience according to unfathomable criteria and requirements' (Culbertson, 1995, p. 169). These unfathomable criteria are one explanation for 'victims' gaining weight to cover up the trauma and finding themselves reliving the trauma as they attempt to reduce weight to the level pertaining when they were traumatised.

A good illustration of the outward display of embodiment is represented in the distinction between the 'civilised' and the 'grotesque' body (Lupton, 1996, p. 19). A civilised body is one that is contained and socially managed and conforms to dominant norms of behaviour, whereas the grotesque body is unruly and less controlled by respectability. Managing and regulating one's emotions has become synonymous with the perceived benefits of rationality and self control, and the extreme example of this is perhaps exhibited in the eating practice of self starvation.

EMOTIONS

Feelings and emotions may be part of the backdrop to our lives or a central and overwhelming dynamic in the pattern of our lives. In Aristotle's inquiry, *The Nicomachean Ethics*, into virtue, character, and the good life, his challenge is to manage our emotional life with intelligence. 'Passions when well exercised can have wisdom, guide thinking, values and survival but they can also go awry' (cited in Goleman, 1997, p. xiv). Candace Pert (1997), who has spent her professional life trying to integrate eastern ideas with science, suggests that the emotions exist in the body as both informational chemicals such as neuropeptides but also in another realm where we experience feeling and inspiration beyond the physical. This unity of mind and body is aptly illustrated by the body blushing red following an embarrassing experience.

PHYSICAL ENVIRONMENT

As we exist bodily, so we are part of a physical world. Sensory qualities attributed to the environment such as temperature, comfort and colour all form an intrinsic part of personal experience. Our senses interact with our physical environment: sights, sounds, smells and tastes, along with significant artefacts, may carry special significance because of associations they have for us. These connections are epitomised in Proust's celebrated evocation of the madeleines and what he calls his inner story:

> as I came home, my mother, seeing that I was cold, offered me some tea, a thing I did not ordinarily take. I declined at first, and then, for no particular reason, changed my mind. She sent out for one of those short, plump little cakes called 'petites madeleines', which look as though they had been moulded in the fluted scallop of a pilgrim's shell. And soon, mechanically, weary after a dull day with the prospect of a depressing morrow, I raised to my lips a spoonful of the tea in which I had soaked a morsel of the cake. No sooner had the warm liquid, and the crumbs with it, touched my palate, a shudder ran through my whole body, and I stopped, intent upon the extraordinary changes that were taking place. An exquisite pleasure had invaded my senses, but individual, detached, with no suggestion of its origin. And at once the vicissitudes of life had become indifferent

to me, its disasters innocuous, its brevity illusory – this new sensation having had on me the effect which love has of filling me with a precious essence; or rather this essence was not in me, it was myself. I had ceased now to feel mediocre, accidental, mortal. Whence could it have come to me, this all-powerful joy? I was conscious that it was connected with the taste of tea and cake, but that it infinitely transcended those savours, could not, indeed, be of the same nature as theirs. Whence did it come? What did it signify? How could I seize upon and define it? (Proust, 2003, p. 101)

SOCIAL CONTEXT

Personal worlds form part of a larger social world. Other people play influential roles in our narrative and in our emotional experience. These others help to create our social worlds and we are enmeshed together in a complex process of mutual definition and construction. Indeed, some people exert greater power of definition over social reality than others, ensuring that we come to assimilate the dominant value system. The medical model of healthcare might be deemed to be one such value system, with allopathic medicine being the dominant system and ayurvedic traditions treated as other.

SENSE OF SELF AND AGENCY

Ethnographers have typically described two contrasting patterns of selfhood referring to the degree of affiliation of a self with its social milieu. Jung (1964) believed that a human being is inwardly whole, but despite losing contact with important parts of our selves, we can reintegrate our different parts if we listen to the messages of our dreams and waking imagination. Individuation is the goal of life, where we harmonise the various components of our psyche. The individuated self is located in the context of the cultural valuation of independence, autonomy and differentiation, whereas the unindividuated self includes a wide variety of significant others (Becker, 1995).

The western view of self is not homogenous and varies among other things with gender and ethnicity, but the idealised self is consistently portrayed as autonomous and unrelated to self fulfilment and key values of authenticity. There is a need to be cautious in considering the self of autobiography as anything more than partial. Neisser (1994, p. 8) draws attention to the oblivious self and talks of the self as a reconstruction, warning that different versions may be conceived everyday.

VALUES AND SEARCH FOR MEANING

The search for meaning and coherence in life gives order and direction to the choices we make about how to live our lives. The point and purpose of our existence has been traditionally found in religion but is also found in the philosophy of reflective people regardless of whether they have a specific religious belief. We weave the stories of our lives to give them meaning but Smith and Sparkes (2002, p. 143) remind us that 'storytellers do coherence through artful practices' that belie the contradictions and distortions in our fragmented lives.

REFLEXIVENESS

Reflexive self awareness is integral to what it is to be human. Not only can the individual exist in multiple identities by being immersed in them, but they can also adopt different perspectives towards themselves by standing back and reflecting. Not only can we think of our own personal world as if it were that of someone else, we can also think of someone else's world as if it were our own. This gives us the capacity for empathy and openness to the idea that other people's worlds may be different from our own.

This theoretical outline of the composition of a personal world attempts to provide a framework within which it is possible to reflect on and examine the stories of others. The illustration that follows should allow you to test out the usefulness of such a framework for yourselves.

A FRAGMENT OF MY PERSONAL WORLD

We begin to understand others when we can imagine ourselves in their world and we make sense of ourselves by weaving stories. I offer below the warp and weft of my own story as I provide some tiny fragments of the continuous flow that has made up my own journey so far. This was written originally for a presentation that included illustrations and allowed intonation in my voice to change the meaning of words but is represented here as an excerpt from the textual form, to give a glimpse of my position in this world we call research.

MIXING ART AND SCIENCE: A BRIDGE OVER TROUBLED WATERS OR A BRIDGE TOO FAR[1]

My journey to belong in the world of research spans five decades. Are these isolated experiences, gaps to be treated with caution, or bridges with spans across memories of feelings, study, books and popular culture that interweave to form a journey of belonging?

---

1 First published as Muncey (2006).

THE JOURNEY

1950s

I stand in the school playground watching my peers playing Fairies and Witches. I know it is a game that involves running around divided into two groups; I do not understand the rules, I am not asked to join in and I don't know how to. I feel excluded and this is my first experience of being an outsider.

1960s

My alienation continues at school. I survive but don't really understand how the mixture of subjects that pitch up in my school calendar relate to each other or make up what I now know is a curriculum. I'm forced to read things that will 'do me good', that bore me and prevented from reading things like comics that interest me.

My home life is a mess but completely hidden from public view and in my head I concoct complicated survival strategies that keep the public and the private both hidden and separate. I leave school at 15, pregnant and alone. By 16, I am married with a child, and very hard up, with one of my most pressing tasks being to invent different ways of disguising mince for meals. I can remember wondering how politics worked, why some people are poor and some rich, and I had my first experience of research.

I went to my GP for a prescription for the contraceptive pill. He tells me I am to be in a research project looking at the effect of the pill. I remember being told he would have to find a person to act as a control and I thought at the time that to find a 17-year-old with an 18-month-old child might be quite tricky. My consent was assumed rather than informed, and I didn't find out the results until exploring years later. The outcome of the research was that the pill was dangerous for some women, but I guess my GP thought it was more important that I didn't get pregnant again rather than having any concerns about me dying.

I go to see Bob Dylan at the Isle of Wight festival and know that I have entered a new era without being told.

1970s

My lot improves in the 1970s. I realise that marriage to a depressed, mixed-up man is rather self destructive and I use my meagre 'O' levels to enter nursing. My first role model remains to this day. Sister M made us serve up gravy to patients in a jug and pour it separately in case they didn't want their dinner swamped with gravy. She would order 15 ml of sherry to help promote the appetites of poorly patients. Her example has stayed with me as the epitome of thoughtful individual care.

I escape the confines of the institution to work in the community. I experience my first taste of sociology. I remember hearing that all children of young single parents wet the bed and go on to become juvenile delinquents. I wait for it to happen; the theory sounds powerful.

As a young keen district nurse I meet Norah, who teaches me the importance of listening and asking the right questions. Norah is in her 80s and has had a leg ulcer for many years. I am hell bent on healing it. Her anxiety increases in direct proportion to the stage of healing. I think she is concerned about my not visiting if the ulcer heals. I anticipate the future paper on the Social Ulcer in about 10 or 15 years time, but in 1976 I only have my naive experience (Wise, 1986). Frustrated by Norah's growing anxiety, I confront her. What is her problem? For years she has had an exudate from the wound which she calls 'the bad' and if it heals, where will all the bad go? She doesn't understand physiology; she has her own system of meaning, and it is a salutary lesson that has stayed with me (Muncey and Parker, 2002).

I first hear 'American Pie', by Don McLean, and I become word perfect without comprehending the lyrics.

1980s

I'm bringing up children in an education system that doesn't seem to fit any better than the one I left. One is dyslexic and will struggle with the effort of reading if it is about his favourite topic of hunting, shooting and fishing and yet he is admonished for not being receptive to extra French lessons at lunchtime. The other is bored and she is rebuked for missing out some maths books, not because she couldn't do the maths, but because the teacher is furious that she missed out a stage without asking. I am left wondering what education is for and about, and encourage my children to follow their hobbies rather than what is deemed 'good for them'.

Professionally, I have entered the world of Health Visiting, where I quickly realise the futility of trying to sell health to people who have no shared concept of what it is. I liken it to the selling of double-glazing, where most people at best ignore you or at worst tell you to go away.

I start to re-engage with the academic world; I balance a degree with perfecting the art of the cheesecake. The boundaries of the subject for me are epitomised by the Stroop phenomenon (Stroop, 1935) and the discovery of George Kelly and Personal Construct Theory (Kelly, 1955). I despaired of ever finding a psychological perspective that felt comfortable with my world view, but Kelly came as close as it gets. The Stroop phenomenon on the other hand is a way of measuring how automatic or intentional some well-practised tasks are and how we respond in conflict situations. The two aspects of cognitive development that are demonstrated by the Stroop task are naming response and counting response. When two responses compete or are in conflict, the time required to make the correct decision is dependent on speed and accuracy. It epitomises the reductionist view of the person.

Kelly on the other hand, from the philosophical standpoint of constructive alternativism, suggests there are no facts in life – there are as many ways of construing an event as people can conceive. The theory's basic assumption is that each person is a scientist whose *raison d'etre* is to develop an increasingly useful model to enable her/him to cope with the world. Kelly suggested that 'nuggets of truth do not lie out there waiting to be discovered' (Kelly, 1970, p. 1). Reality is constructed reality, it is negoti-ated and contested, it is provisional and subject to revision. Kelly's criterion of good research is not its validity or its reliability; it is its viability, its fertility in the business of living. Kelly's scientist is an ordinary human being, engaged in the most natural of all human activities – enquiry. Kelly's refreshing view entered the world in 1955 and yet was mostly ignored until the 1970s.

Kelly was very aware himself of the subversive nature of his ideas. First, in con-trast to traditional research, Kelly does not separate the author from its subjects. His principle of reflexivity puts researcher and researched in the same universe of dis-course. Kelly himself was one of the pioneers of unconventional methods of asking questions; he focused on what is inarticulate and on those whose voices go unheard. For me, there is no competition, the fascinating world of Kelly far outweighs the contribution of the Stroop phenomenon, but a paradoxical part of me loved doing the experiments.

I might have stayed with Kelly. Indeed I considered offering him up as the ultimate mixed method. Repertory grids give unique individual perceptions of the world while generating quantitative data to keep the most extreme rationalist happy.

I've discovered *Jonathon Livingstone Seagull* (Bach, 1973), and Kahlil Gibran's (1980) *The Prophet*. I'm entering an existential world before I know the meaning of the word, but it frees me from the memories of literature at school and I start to feel liberated.

1990s

A feminist itch needs scratching at the beginning of the 1990s. With that wonderful synchronicity in life that I have come to respect and rely on, a masters degree in women's studies is waiting locally for my attention. For the first time, I question the conventional approaches to what knowledge is, a knowledge system that appeared to exclude the meaning of the lived experience of many people whose stories lie outside the contrived world of empirical research. For the first time, I found people allowing me to express a view without telling me I was wrong or misguided. It was not wrong to be passionately interested in something simply because I had personal experience of it. For the first time, I realised that we don't just learn from formal historical events, but from subjective feelings and thoughts with which we experience the events of our everyday lives; and so it was that I started to examine why I had never felt a 'proper' nurse or a 'proper' mother.

It was at this time I started to attend conferences and to listen to the many and varied explanations put forward to explain the cause, side effects and solutions to teenage pregnancy. I was fascinated by the studies that attempted to explain the rea-sons for, and lived experience of, the pregnant adolescent and realised they were not telling my story.

'American Pie' is re-released and a hit all over again. This time I have a Brunerian 'aha' experience. '*Drove my Chevy to the levee but the levee was dry*' were words I could sing word perfectly but never really understood. Juxtaposed with hearing the song again is a news item about the levees' being flooded down the Mississippi. This becomes an anecdote in my teaching on developing curricula about the length of time some things take to learn and therefore the futility of doing educational evaluations too soon.

The early 1990s are characterised by death: the suicide of my oldest friend and the death of my father. I embark on a course called 'Life and Death'; note the ambiguities in my own views about abortion, suicide, capital punishment and euthanasia. I conclude that death itself is a red herring. It is suffering that is the crux of the matter.

By the end of the 1990s I have read the *Celestine Prophecy* (Redfield, 1994). It sparks an interest in a world beyond conventional explanations and I add 'New Age' to the growing list of concepts that appear to alienate me from the academic world.

I read books that give me more insight into real life issues than do academic texts, and I start to recommend them to my students. I recommend *Paddy Clarke Ha Ha Ha* by Roddy Doyle (1993) to anyone who wants to understand how a child might feel when his father leaves. It takes you into the mind of a child in a way that, for me, phenomenological studies don't.

I never got the chance to run away. I was too late. He left first, The way the door shut; he didn't slam it. Something; I just knew: he wasn't coming back. He just closed it, like he was going down to the shops, except it was the front door and we only used the front door when people came. He didn't slam it. He closed it behind him – I saw him in the glass. He waited for a few seconds, then went. He didn't have a suitcase or even a jacket, but I knew. (Doyle, 1993, p. 280)

2000s

A craving to be included in the academic community culminated in a doctoral study that paradoxically marked the end of my need to conform. All of my discomfort with received wisdom is finding solace in answers from outside mainstream evidence. The paradigm shift that I feel is occurring in the world is reflected in the shift in my own views to find solutions outside conventional approaches.

The climb up the academic ladder allowed me to understand how knowledge is generated and the power structures that are in place to perpetuate certain claims. I recognise that expert knowledge is socially sanctioned in a way that common sense knowledge is usually not, and the various practices that are accorded higher or lower status dependent on how it has been produced and who is saying it. So at the same time as learning the rules of the research game, my own story became entwined with what I was reading and hearing and I started to notice that the expert voices were not telling my story.

The puzzle over deviancy or otherwise of my individual case gives me further cause to reflect on how many other truths are denied. This presents a recurring philosophical idea in my patchwork life, namely, what is truth? Whose truth is valuable? Can truth vary? Is an experience true if it corresponds with the facts, or is there an absolute truth that depends on the consistency of the whole? Research has never been very successful in accepting new ideas that don't conform to received wisdom, hence the proliferation of theory to support false memory syndrome (FMS) (Lynn and Payne, 1997; Laurence et al., 1998). Rather than accept the harsh reality, that some women damaged by sexual abuse may be telling the truth, FMS conveys a powerful expert voice to silence the weakened victim.

In vain attempts to detail the inner cognitive processes, memory researchers epitomised by Kihlstrom (1998) introduce ideas such as 'exhumed memory': the exhumation of repressed memories, particularly associated with forms of abuse but clearly more concerned with issues of truth and reality. This appears to support the idea that a memory, thought to be long forgotten, must be considered a lie unless historical evidence can be found to support it.

By now I have been inspired by Chopra's (1990) *Quantum Healing*, where I find a fascinating proposal that the intelligence of the body is much better able to heal itself, and I find a confidence to write my own papers to see if anyone else agrees with my way of thinking. In one particular paper I write of my growing frustration with my students' battle with phenomenology. I ask 'is the philosophical angst of phenomenology really worth the effort?' and reach the conclusion that really it isn't (Muncey, 2004). Phenomenologists suggest that life is separated between everyday life (structured by habits) and 'provinces of meaning', where we reflect on everyday life.

Take, for example the difference between the meaning **of** life and finding meaning **in** life. We either take on the simple truth that God is the provider of life and all its sacred rituals; or at the other extreme, in 'His or her' absence, like the existentialist Camus, we liken it to rolling a stone up hill, only to find it rolling down again with monotonous regularity (Camus, 2000). Asking people to talk about the meaning of any 'lived experience' is a similar philosophical quest. I would suggest that what novice phenomenological researchers may be doing is asking what makes particular experiences meaningful. One is asking them to philosophise and the other to tell their story by describing meaningful events.

As my children leave home I am drawn to fill a gap in my life. You perhaps won't be surprised, in the light of my friend's suicide in the last decade, that I become a Samaritan. Here, I learn about the dreariness and staggering loneliness in people's mixed up lives. I am faced with many contradictions. I remember Durkheim's (1982a) *Rules of Sociological Method*: explanation requires comparison; comparison requires classification; classification requires the definition of those facts to be classified, compared, and ultimately explained. Consistent with these rules, Durkheim (1982b, p. 42) began his 1897 work with an insistence that

> our first task ... must be to determine the order of facts to be studied under the name of suicide ... we must inquire whether, among the different varieties of death, some have common qualities objective enough to be recognized by all honest observers.

Durkheim's rules specifically suppress the presence of actual people so that objectivity and honesty can prevail. Compare this with an excerpt from one of the characters in Hornby's (2005) book *A Long Way Down*

> I'd spent the previous couple of months looking up suicide inquests on the internet, just out of curiosity. And nearly every single time, the coroner says the same thing: 'He took his life while the balance of his mind was disturbed.' And then you read the story about the poor bastard: his wife was sleeping with his best friend, he's lost his job, his daughter had been killed in a road accident some months before … Hello, Mr Coroner? Anyone at home? I'm sorry, but there's no disturbed mental balance here, my friend. I'd say he got it just right. Bad thing upon bad thing until you can't take any more, and then it's off to the nearest multi-story car park in the family hatchback with a length of rubber tubing. Surely that's fair enough? Surely the coroner's inquest should read, 'He took his own life after sober and careful contemplation of the fucking shambles it had become'? (Hornby, 2005, p. 7)

Hornby's description in the words of his character resonates with the experiences I have heard from the suicidal.

Finally, after three decades I discover that 'American Pie' is autobiographical (Dearborn, 1972). The reason it resonates is that it depicts an era that I am familiar with and people that are part of my history. This resonance links me to a time and place and validates my identity.

A BRIDGE TOO FAR?

Finally, I come full circle to the present day; the latest bridge in my thinking comes from a workshop I attend at a conference where I am introduced to the work of Mikhail Bakhtin. Bakhtin provides my bridge between art and science. He is known as a social thinker as well as a literary critic. He trained as a scholar in the philological tradition in which the study of language and literature is inextricably linked, and his work parallels the current reawakening of interest in the everyday world. His is one of several modern epistemologies that seek to grasp human behaviour through the use humans make of language. Holquist (2002, p. 30) suggests that Bakhtin uses 'the literary genre of the novel as an allegory for representing existence as the condition of authoring'. An authoring of the unique place I occupy in existence looks very much like an autoethnographic text.

Full Circle

This text ended at a point in 2005. Since then a myriad of further books, films, dreams and conversations have added to my world view. I retired from work only to find that work didn't stop. I have started to ponder on the extent to which anyone has more than one identity, more than one story, and I remain fascinated by the myriad of individuals who make up my world.

Summary

- Specific consciousness and multiple worlds: the self is a collection of ever-changing experiences tied together by such relationships as a physical body and a memory.
- Time and space: all narrative will represent a flow of experiences, actions and events, a distillation of life so far coupled with an anticipation of the future.
- Embodiment: our senses cannot function independently of our bodies.
- Emotions: emotions exist in the body both as informational chemicals and also in another realm where we experience feeling and inspiration beyond the physical.
- Physical environment: sensory qualities form an intrinsic part of the personal experience.
- Social context: other people play influential roles in our narrative and some come to be associated with a dominant value system.
- Sense of self and agency: the western view of self is not homogenous and varies among other things with gender and ethnicity; but the idealised self is consistently portrayed as autonomous and unrelated, with self fulfilment and authenticity as key values.
- Values and search for meaning: coherence and meaning are found in reflection.
- Reflexiveness: multiple identities and reflexivity give us the capacity for empathy and entry to another's world of meaning.

And from the example given:

- Self is a process not a structure. The process of becoming is always in motion. Any evocation of an experience is always incomplete and in transition, and at best can only be described as a snapshot.
- The self, the individual, is a highly reflexive, historically positioned entity, who attempts to engage in meaningful relationships with their culture, their society and other individuals. Like an iceberg, only a fraction of them is visible and autoethnography attempts to increase this visibility to provide a wider range of stories for individuals to connect with.
- Autoethnographies need to be organised around certain features: portrayal of the self, one's positioning in the world, the interaction of the experience of self in a particular world and the ways in which we come to organise experience and our actions.
- If consciousness is not a direct copy of the world then metaphor is an excellent vehicle for unfolding experience.

FURTHER READING

Coffey, Amanda (1999) *The Ethnographic Self: Fieldwork and the representation of identity.* Sage, London.

For further consideration of the iterative relationship between the researcher and the field, Coffey's text draws attention to the creation of the ethnographic self and the embodiment of the field and the self.

Freshwater, Dawn (2002) *Therapeutic Nursing: Improving patient care through self awareness and reflection.* Sage, London.

Chapter 1 gives an excellent overview of the theories of self, and links to recent debates about the challenges to seeing the self as a unified set of experiences.

REFERENCES

Bach, R. (1973) *Jonathan Livingston Seagull.* Avon Books, New York.

Becker, A.E. (1995) *Body, Self and Society: The view from Fiji.* University of Pennsylvania Press, Philadelphia, PA.

Blackmore, S. (2001) State of the Art: Consciousness. *The Psychologist,* **14**(10), 522–5.

Camus, A. (2000) *The Myth of Sisyphus.* Penguin, Harmondsworth.

Chopra, D. (1990) *Quantum Healing: Exploring the frontiers of mind/body medicine.* Bantum Books, New York.

Cooley, C. (1902) *Human Nature and Social Order.* Shocken, New York.

Culbertson, R. (1995) Embodied memory, transcendence, and telling: Recounting trauma, re-establishing the self. *New Literary History,* **26**(1), 169–95.

Dearborn, B. (1972) Bob Dearborn's American Pie Special. Retrieved 11 August 2009, from http://user.pa.net/~ejjeff/pie.html.

Doyle, R. (1993) *Paddy Clarke Ha Ha Ha.* Vintage, London.

Durkheim, E. (1982a) *The Rules of the Sociological Method.* Free Press, New York.

Durkheim, E. (1982b [1897]) *Suicide: A study in sociology.* The Free Press of Glenco, New York.

Foucault, M. (1988) Technologies of the Self. In L. Martin, H. Gutman and P. Hatton (Eds) *Technologies of the Self: A seminar with Michael Foucault.* Tavistock, London.

Gallagher, S. and Shear, J. (Eds.) (1999) *Models of the Self.* Imprint Academic, Thorverton, Devon.

Gibran, K. (1980) *The Prophet.* Heinemann, London.

Goleman, D. (1997) *Emotional Intelligence.* Bantam Books, London.

Grosz, E. (1990) Inscriptions and Body Maps: Representations and the corporeal. In T. Threadgold and A. Cranny-Francis (Eds) *Feminine/Masculine and Representation.* Allen and Unwin, Sydney, NSW.

Holquist, M. (2002) *Dialogism: Bakhtin and his world.* Routledge, London.

Hornby, N. (2005) *A Long Way Down.* Quality Paperbacks Direct, Chatham.

James, W. (1890) *The Principles of Psychology.* Holt, New York.

Jaynes, J. (1979) *The Origin of Consciousness in the Breakdown of the Bicameral Mind.* Allen Lane, London.

Jung, C.G. (1964) *A Man and his Symbols.* Aldus Books, London.

Kelly, G. (1955) *The Psychology of Personal Constructs.* Norton, New York.

Kelly, G. (1970) A Brief Introduction to Personal Construct Theory. In D. Bannister (Ed.) *Perspectives in Personal Construct Theory.* Academic Press, London.

Kihlstrom, J. (1998) Exhumed Memory. In S. Lynn and K. McConkey (Eds) *Truth in Memory.* Guilford Press, New York.

Laurence, J-R., Day, D. and Gaston, L. (1998) From Memories of Abuse to Abuse of Memories. In S. Lynn and K. McConkey (Eds) *Truth in Memory.* Guilford Press, New York.

Lupton, D. (1996) *Food, the Body and the Self.* Sage, London.

Lynn, S. and Payne, D. (1997) Memory as the theater of the past: The psychology of false memories. *Current Directions,* **6**, 55.

Mead, G. (1934) *Mind, Self and Society.* University of Chicago Press, Chicago, IL.

Merleau-Ponty, M. (1962) *Phenomenology of Perception.* Routledge and Kegan Paul, London.

Muncey, T. (2004) Is the Philosophical Angst of Phenomenology Really Worth the Effort? In *Advances in Qualitative Methods.* University of Alberta, Edmonton, AB.

Muncey, T. (2006) A bridge over troubled waters or a bridge too far. *Journal of Research in Nursing,* **11**(3), 223–33.

Muncey, T. and Parker, A. (Eds) (2002) *Chronic Disease Management: A practical guide.* Palgrave, Basingstoke.

Neisser, U. (1994) Self Narratives: True and false. In U. Neisser and V. Fivush (Eds) *The Remembering Self.* Cambridge University Press, Cambridge.

Nettleton, S. and Watson, J. (1998) Introduction. In S. Nettleton and J. Watson (Eds) *The Body in Everyday Life.* Routledge, London.

Pert, C.B. (1997) *Molecules of Emotion: Why you feel the way you feel.* Simon and Schuster, London.

Polkinghorne, D. (1998) *Narrative Knowing and the Human Sciences.* State University of New York Press, New York.

Proust, M. (2003) *In Search of Lost Time: The way by Swanns.* Penguin, Harmondsworth.

Redfield, J. (1994) *The Celestine Prophecy.* Bantam Books, London.

Romanyshyn, R. (1982) *Psychological Life: From science to metaphor.* The Open University Press, Milton Keynes.

Shilling, C. (1993) *The Body and Social Theory.* Sage, London.

Smith, B. and Sparkes, A.C. (2002) Men, sport, spinal cord injury and the construction of coherence: Narrative practice in action. *Qualitative research,* **2**(2), 143–71.

Stroop, J.R. (1935) Studies of interference in serial verbal reactions. *Journal of Experimental Psychology,* **18**, 643–62.

Wise, E. (1986) The social ulcer. *Nursing Times,* **82**(21), 47–9.

3
WHAT IS AUTOETHNOGRAPHY? MAKING SENSE OF INDIVIDUAL EXPERIENCE

CHAPTER PREVIEW

So you now have some sense of what elements make up your personal world and you might be ready to include your story in your work; but where does all this fit into the world of research methods? Who else is writing about and using these approaches and indeed, what are some of the alternatives that you might consider?

Justification for a particular approach is an important part of the research process, particularly when the sample involves small numbers of people. I am intrigued by the concern of those that promote the randomised control trial (RCT) as the gold standard for research. By implication, anything less than a rigorous RCT with large samples and rigorous control of variables produces evidence of an inferior quality that cannot be used to inform policy or practice. Somehow, a claim of subjectivity is enough to render an individual story an inferior type of evidence. Elsewhere (Muncey, 2009), I argue that subjectivity/objectivity is a false dichotomy and that far from being a gold standard the RCT places too much control over internal validity at the expense of what Neisser (1976) calls 'ecological validity'.

I'll begin now to introduce you to the ways in which individual stories have been utilised in research. This should help provide a practical and philosophical justification for the portrayal of individual experience as an important contribution to research that adopts social science methodologies.

WHAT ARE THE SOCIAL SCIENCES FOR?

Social science is, in its broadest sense, the study of society and the manner in which people behave and impact on the world around us (ESRC, 2008). While many people are not aware of the impact of social science research, many researchers 'think they know something about society worth telling to others' (Becker, 1986, p. 122).

Reviews of the state of social science research have increasingly focused on the relevance and utility of the way in which research is disseminated (Rhind, 2003). This is in response to what has sometimes been referred to as the 'so what' factor in which research has been criticised, both by those within the field and by the public at large. The criticism is for not engaging sufficiently with the methodological and ethical challenges of transferring the value of social science research relevantly and meaningfully into arenas in which it could make a productive difference (Polkinghorne, 2004, p. 38).

The conceptual, ethical and methodological challenges are far-ranging and include questions such as 'What kind and level of responsibility do researchers take for mediating the productive dissemination and use of their research?' and 'What are the methodological challenges of disseminating research to different audiences and interest groups?' (Todres, 1998; Gray, 2000; Halling, 2002). Jones (2006, p. 67) suggests that by 'rethinking our relationships within communities and across disciplines, we are presented with opportunities to move beyond imitation of "scientistic" reports in dissemination of our work and look towards means of (re)presentation that embrace the humanness of social science pursuits'. The term 're-presentation of findings' refers to a three-fold process in which, as mediators of understanding, qualitative researchers care for their informants' voices, care for the complexity and contextuality of the phenomena being expressed, and care for the research audience (Todres, 2000).

The use of creative methods with concomitant creative representations in publications goes someway to addressing these issues. However, if the act of living is 'a performance with all the twists and turns of plot and sub plot, journeys complete and incomplete, with a cast of characters all with their own particular versions and standpoints', can this be turned into a written account (Muncey and Robinson, 2007, p. 80)? Or equally is the written account the most appropriate? Non-linguistic forms of the arts for representing research data, such as performance, are becoming more possible with the advent of CDs and electronic journals. Barone and Eisner (2006) suggest that, although non-linguistic forms represent the greatest challenge to representing research data and are therefore methodologically contentious, they enhance perspectives pertaining to certain human activities, and broaden and deepen ongoing conversations.

Spry (2001, p. 727) suggests that 'human experience ... is chaotic and messy requiring a pluralism of discursive and interpretive methods'. The text and the body that generates it cannot be separated. Rob Robinson takes experience and both literally and metaphorically writes it through and on the body when he writes performatively about his experience of living with psychosis and the tattoos that for him represent his journey to recovery (Muncey and Robinson, 2007). This makes it a corporeal experience that rejects the notion that 'lived experience can only be represented indirectly through quotations from field notes, observations or interviews' (Denzin, 1992a, p. 20). In autoethnographic methods, the researcher is the epistemological and ontological nexus upon which the research process turns (Spry, 2001, p. 711).

MESSY WORLDS

Law (2003, p. 3) considers the research establishment's discomfort with messy worlds. He writes

> sometimes I think of it as a form of hygiene. Do your methods properly. Eat your epistemological greens. Wash your hands after mixing with the real world. Then you will lead the good research life. Your data will be clean. Your findings warrantable. The product you will produce will be pure. Guaranteed to have a long shelf-life.

I would argue that in our attempts to achieve internal validity in research at the expense of ecological validity, the complexity of individual experiences gets lost in the wash.

Researchers try to find ways of expressing the messiness of social science research. Rapport et al. (2005) talk about the need to explore new territories from which to look for more freedom of expression. They define these new territories as being seated within 'Edgelands' – a transitional area between established and new methods, from which one can concentrate on the process of discovery while retaining a sense of the unknown. Rapport et al. (2005, p. 38) comment that: 'This interface provides a space in which new approaches can develop. It represents a territory in which new theories can be approached and new ways of asking and answering questions can be found'. They use a fascinating metaphor from Marion Shoard (cited in Rapport et al., 2005, p. 37) who, on writing about the British landscape, reflects:

> We are aware of the great conurbations. But not of the edgelands ... Between urban and rural stands a kind of landscape quite different from either ... Often characterised by rubbish tips, superstores and gypsy encampments ... for most of us most of the time this mysterious no man's land passes unnoticed in our imaginations, it barely exists ... But if we fail to attend to the activity of the interface we forfeit the chance not only to shape ... change but also to influence the effects of it on other parts of the environment.

DEFINING AUTOETHNOGRAPHY

Autoethnographers reside comfortably within these edgelands and relish the interface between the different landscapes, although they also want to belong in the academy. At the beginning of many autoethnographic papers is the accustomed salute to the founding thinkers and writers in the field. I am surrounded by the seminal texts in this field as I write and ponder on the rationale for a selection of definitions. I find myself in agreement with Gingrich-Philbrook (2005, pp. 301, 311) who, despite reassurances of his interest and participation in autoethnography, finds himself

> contesting the conversational observations of others that autoethnography legitimates its knowledge by adding cultural critique to autobiography ... personally I think they are wasting their time, I swear to God if I read one more essay attempting to justify the presence of the self in writing to the patriarchal council of self-satisfied social scientists I'll well, I could say 'Scream' or 'go to Wal-mart ... I think I'll put it this way: if I read one more essay blah blah blah, I think I'll put it down'.

However, it would be distinctly unhelpful in a text proposing to educate the uninitiated autoethnographer not to select a few to give a flavour of the thinking and provide a starting place for positioning oneself. So the four I have selected reflect my own adventure into this area.

> *1) an autobiographical genre of writing and research that displays multiple layers of consciousness, connecting the personal to the cultural.* (Ellis and Bochner, 2000, p. 739)

At a time when I was pondering on the role of the individual in research in respect of my own story and that of a key individual in my PhD, I attended a conference and heard Carolyn Ellis deliver a paper, now published and called 'He*art*ful autoethnography' (Ellis, 1999). This became a turning point in my thinking about individual stories and it is therefore not surprising that my first quote reflects her stance. Although it is fair to say that Ellis and Bochner (2000) also note that, because autoethnography has such a wide array of textual practice, it is impossible and undesirable to arrive at a single definition. In terms of this definition, though, you might want to consider to what extent it is possible to disconnect the personal from the cultural, as if the two were not completely entwined and, given the scarcity of understanding about consciousness, what do they mean by multiple layers?

> *2) an ethnography that includes the researcher's vulnerable self, emotions, body and spirit and produces evocative stories that create the effect of reality and seeks fusion between social science and literature. It also questions the notion of a coherent, individual self.* (Reed-Danahay, 1997)

This second one gives slightly more detail about some of the aspects of personal experience that might be considered worthy of further exposition, and highlights the relationship between art and science that promotes 'evocative stories'. But what does she mean by 'the effect of reality'? Like 'truth', 'reality' is a suspicious concept. The notion of one version of reality is contested, so isn't it possible that the evocative story is the reality for that person, even though it may not concur with the 'reality' of someone else?

I have also begun to think more about the notion of a coherent individual self. Proust (2003), in his autobiographical writing, refers to the idea of the inner story. To demonstrate that illustrations can come equally from text that sets out to be fiction, I will introduce you to a short extract of fictional short story writing called 'Gardening Guerillas' (Stevenson, 2006). In the story, Alice is a 70-year-old widow who is caught up in a bitter feud with her son and daughter-in-law, who want her to move out of her house of 43 years and into a retirement home so they can move into her home. Eventually accepting the inevitable move, she plans to sabotage her beautiful garden with pernicious plants that will wreak a slow revenge. As she sets about selecting and buying the plants, she meets up with an old flame who clearly understands her better than does her son. She explains to him: 'you can talk to someone who's from your own background and your own generation in a way you can't talk to anyone else ... it's not personal affinity ... it's the shape and size of your unexamined assumptions' (Stevenson, 2006, p. 204).

Because so many points of reference are required to fully appreciate a point of view, it is necessary for the autoethnographer to make allowances for this in their creation. Coherence suggests unity, rationality, logic, lucidity and reason. Because Alice's son cannot understand what it might be like to have to leave a garden that one has been tending for a lifetime, the slow revenge epitomises the extent of her simmering anger. It is emotional, not logical or rational, something that can easily be understood by someone who intimately knows her, and the chronology of her life and times. There is no coherence between the passionate gardener and her use of the garden to wreak revenge, but together they portray a multidimensional character in the story.

Bayard (2008, p. 82) picks up this idea of an inner story, which he defines as 'a set of mythic representations either collective or individual, that come between the reader and any new piece of writing'. In order to connect with people we need to understand these inner stories. So for me the shape and size of unexamined assumptions is a key feature of an autoethnographic piece, but I suspect real resonance with the experience can only occur if there is some connection to the time, place and historical setting of the experience. Perhaps a crucial component of the 'success' of a piece is that the mythic representations are made explicit. In discussions about my own story of being a teenage mother I have often had to explain to a younger audience that my pregnancy occurred at a historical juncture, when abortion was still illegal and when pregnancy outside marriage was still a shameful event. This often leads to discussion about how my story connects with young girls getting pregnant today, when neither of those assumptions are quite the same.

> 3) *a self narrative that critiques the situations of self with others in social contexts.* (Spry, 2001, p. 710)

Tami Spry introduced me to the idea that what makes autoethnography different from normal autobiographies is that an autoethnographic account should attempt to subvert a dominant discourse. First-person accounts of personal experience, and their claims regarding truth, knowledge and values, are typically framed in terms of pre-existing 'master narratives' (Mishler, 1984; Boje, 1991); 'dominant discourses' (Gee, 1992; Gergen, 1995); or 'cultural texts' (Denzin, 1992b). These master narratives have the appearance of reflections of the world as it 'actually' is, rather than mediating interpretive frameworks. 'Master narratives possess a totalizing character as they aim to impose order on the world from a distinct, if often hidden, ideological point of view, one that appears to be authoritative, final, exclusionary of alternative viewpoints, all-knowing' (Barone, 2008, p. 38).

Master narratives derive from tradition, and they typically constrain narratives of personal experience, because they hold the narrator to culturally given standards, to taken-for-granted notions of what is good and what is wrong. At the same time, because the propositions implicit in master narratives or dominant discourses are widely accepted as self-evident, narrators who cast their own account in terms deriving from such a discourse are free to present the personal story as a description of events that is synonymous with 'reality'. Therefore, there is no need to define or reason about the claims implicit in one's account, nor is one expected to legitimate these claims. This is evident in statements where there is an often unspoken 'it's obvious isn't it …' or 'of course I take it for granted that …' an implicit acceptance of the taken for grantedness of an assumption that doesn't need to be explained or indeed might even be unconsciously hidden in the psyche of the person telling the story. An example might be that 'all children need fathers', an unquestioning assumption that belies the contribution of decades of psychological evidence and the sociological implications of the family in a capitalist society.

> 4) *The poetic essay is … an imaginative construction whose truth lies not in its facticity but in its evocative potentiality.* (Pelias, 1999, p. xiv)

However, our experiences are not just stories, they are lives; experiences, performances, 'embodied stories, (which) makes the cultural conflict concrete' (Langellier, 1999, p. 208). The performance of an embodied story is complicated by its gaps and omissions and is uncomfortable to hear. The challenge is how to reach an audience to subvert the dominant discourse.

Performance can be seen as the embodiment of story. Pelias (1999, pp. 109, 110) describes performance as a 'way of knowing … an act of becoming, a strategy for discovering oneself by trying on scripts to test their fit' and a 'method of understanding, bodily located in the experience of doing'.

Tami Spry's 'From Goldilocks to Dreadlocks: Hair raising tales of racializing bodies' is a good example of performance autoethnography. Not only does Tami write about master narratives of whiteness and womanhood, she lives out the experience by growing her hair into dreadlocks. She explains that autoethnographic performance 'can provide a space for the emancipation of the voice and body from homogenizing knowledge production and academic discourse structures' (Spry, 2001, p. 727).

ORIGINS OF AUTOETHNOGRAPHY

The origins of autoethnography arise in the field of anthropology and the ways in which anthropologists wrote ethnographies of their own people. One of the first references to autoethnography in academic literature is by Hayano (1979). He reports on a seminar he attended in 1966, where Sir Raymond Firth in a seminar on structuralism made reference to Jomo Kenyatta's study of his native Kikuyu people. Seemingly, when Kenyatta presented his field material in one of Malinowski's seminars, a heated debate ensued with another Kikuyu speaker who happened to be the white South African, L.S.B. Leakey. Whilst the exact nature of their differences of opinion were never clarified, their argument raises questions about 'judging the validity of anthropological data by assessing the characteristics, interests, and origin of the person who did the fieldwork' (Hayano, 1979, p. 100). Hayano develops this idea further to include his criteria for autoethnography, which are summarised as follows:

- some prior knowledge of the people, their culture and language
- ability to be accepted to some degree or to pass as a native member.

Included in his typology for autoethnography were ethnographers who had studied their own cultural, social, ethnic, racial, religious, residential or sex membership group or combinations of these categories. The other main group were researchers who had acquired an intimate familiarity with certain sub-cultural, recreational or occupational groups. What he excluded were the writings of many anthropologists who conducted participant observation research among a distinctly different group than their own. As he states, 'no matter how exhaustive Malinowski's knowledge of Trobiand island society was, he could never be considered a native by his or their standards' (Hayano, 1979, p. 100).

PARADIGMATIC CONCERNS

Hayano (1979, p. 101) raises an issue that still resonates in the academic community today. Although he suggests that the final products of autoethnography have not followed one common paradigm or one distinctive theoretical framework, there are always a 'number of major stumbling blocks to paradigmatic change in any science, and these relate directly to the social organisation and politics of academic scholarship and information dissemination'. Reports of autoethnographic studies have struggled to find a place for their dissemination in the academic world although, as reported later, there has been an increase in the number of papers published in the last five years.

INSIDER RESEARCH

Most concerns about insider research are about the blurred relationships between the researcher and researched, which may lead to problems with reliability and validity (Borbasi, 1994); although Rudge (1996) emphasises that one of the strengths of being an insider is an awareness of the history behind the research questions.

An individual insider does not necessarily contain an unchallengeable 'truth', as there as many different interpretations of events and behaviour among individuals in the same group which may be contradictory. Indeed, insiders may be blind to the taken-for-granted assumptions about social behaviour that are ' the hazards of intimate familiarity' (Hayano, 1979, p. 102).

PHILOSOPHICAL STANCE

I struggled for a while to find a satisfactory philosophy that united art and science until I stumbled upon the writings of Mikhail Bakhtin. Bakhtin's ideas contribute to the idea of a human science through his writing about the theory of the novel. Gaining insight into what it is to be human comes from many sources. Books and popular culture have proved to be some of my most successful bridges into other ways of thinking; from them I have learned the skills inherent in creating autoethnographic accounts. Bakhtin's ideas support Ellis's (1999, p. 669) suggestion that autoethnography connects 'the practices of social science with the living of life'.

The characteristics that Bakhtin suggested were prerequisites of a realist novel could also be described as the prerequisites for an autoethnography: (1) the novels should not be 'poetic', as the word poetic is used in other genres of imaginative literature; (2) the hero of a novel should not be heroic in either the epic or the tragic sense of the word: he should combine in himself negative as well as positive features, low as well as lofty, ridiculous as well as serious; (3) the hero should not be portrayed as an already completed and unchanging person, but as one who is evolving and developing, a person who learns from life; (4) the novel should become for the contemporary world what the epic was for the ancient world (Bakhtin, 1981, p. 10).

DIALOGISM

Bakhtin is interesting because he anticipated a number of later developments in post-structuralist and postmodernist theory, which have been part of the broad assault on the axiom of western science and rationality. All sociocultural phenomena, according to Bakhtin, are constituted through the ongoing, dialogical relationship between individuals and groups. This involves a multiplicity of different languages, discourse and symbolising practices and most importantly privileges the 'marginal, the de-centred, the contingent and the unofficial' (Gardiner and Bell, 1998, p. 5). Bakhtin suggests that the most important events in life are not the grand, dramatic or catastrophic, but the apparently small and prosaic ones of everyday life. He awakened an interest in the everyday world. He referred to the 'unfinalizable' nature of the thoughts and actions of human subjects with respect to what he called 'events of Being' (Gardiner and Bell, 1998, p. 5).

Bakhtin's theory of dialogic relates to the constant, endless state of intentional and value-laden dialogue into which every word enters, and to heteroglossia, the diversity and stratification of languages, or 'many languagedness' within society (Holquist, 2002, p. 1). For Bakhtin, the self is an embodied entity situated in concrete time and space, which is constituted in and through its dialogical relations with others and the world at large. The term dialogue has many meanings in his work. As a global concept, it refers to a concept of 'truth' as a conversation rather than a series of propositions. He places a considerable premium on

> human creativity, responsibility and agency and in the dialogical relationship between language and other social processes are practices that are simultaneously structured and structuring: hence human beings are not simply 'effects' of linguistic systems of apparatuses of power/knowledge, as many post modernists would have it. (Gardiner and Bell, 1998, p. 6)

Bakhtin also gives me a justification for using autobiography in the world of 'research': he suggests that stories 'are the means by which values are made coherent in particular situations' (Holquist, 2002, p. 37).

CURRENT DEBATES

In the last 20 years, there has been a growth in research outputs described as auto-ethnographic. In preparing to write this book, I have maintained a link to the publications identified by the keyword autoethnography on the Web of Science database. Overall, 162 items have been published. Between 1990 and 2002, this never rose above five items. From 2003, the number rose considerably, up to 35 items per year. In terms of the number of citations of autoethnographic papers in the 1990s, this was never above ten, with an increase in 2008 of 43 citations. This demonstrates the increased interest in this genre of research, but it is still relatively small when compared with a search with the keyword 'narrative', which in 2008 produced 2321 papers, or for 'phenomenology' 1277 papers.[1]

Autoethnography in its present form is often thought to be synonymous with 'evocative autoethnography'. As this genre of research has developed, it has moved further away from its anthropological origins and drawn on postmodern sensibilities.

EVOCATIVE AUTOETHNOGRAPHY

As previously stated, my introduction to autoethnography was Carolyn Ellis perform- ing 'He*art*ful Autoethnography' at a conference in 1999. She was aiming to 'extend ethnography to include the heart, the autobiographical and the artistic text' (Ellis, 1999, p. 669). Her evocative performance captured my imagination and I started to see how the researcher's vulnerable self could connect the practices of social science with the living of life.

In this excerpt from 'He*art*ful Autoethnography' Carolyn is challenged by a PhD student who has come to ask her to supervise her thesis on the grounds that she can't find anyone else to supervise a qualitative study and she thinks Carolyn is interested in grounded theory (Ellis, 1999, pp. 671–2).

> 'I don't do grounded theory much anymore,' I say. 'Most of what I do is autoethnography.'
> 'Autoethnography? What's that?' she asks, writing the word on her notepad as she looks at me.
> 'Well, I start with my personal life. I pay attention to my physical feelings, thoughts and emotions. I use what I call systematic sociological introspection and emotional recall to try to understand an experience I've lived through. Then I write my experience as a story. By exploring a particular life, I hope to understand a way of life.'
> 'So you just write about your life?' Sylvia says casually. 'That doesn't sound too difficult.'
> I turn around; stare at her for a moment as though I'll get a sign as to whether I should promote autoethnography to Sylvia. When no sign is forthcoming, I say, 'Oh, it's amaz- ingly difficult. It's certainly not something that most people can do well. Most social scientists don't write well enough to carry it off. Or they're not sufficiently introspec- tive about their feelings or motives or the contradictions they experience. Ironically, many aren't observant enough of the world around them. The self-questioning autoethnography demands is extremely difficult. So is confronting things about yourself that are less than flattering. Believe me, honest autoethnographic exploration generates a lot of fears and self-doubts – and emotional pain. Just when you think you can't stand the pain anymore, well that's when the real work has only begun. Then there's the vulnerability of revealing yourself, not being able to take back what you've

---

1 These figures are produced by analysis of the search results in ISI Web of Knowledge.

written or having any control over how readers interpret it. It's hard not to feel your life is being critiqued as well as your work. It can be humiliating. And the ethical issues,' I warn, 'just wait until you're writing about family members and loved ones who are part of your story.' Sylvia holds on to her chair, her eyes wide. I smile and let out the breath I've been holding. 'I'm sorry. I get really passionate about all this,' I say more gently. 'Of course, there are rewards, too: For example, you come to understand yourself in deeper ways. And with understanding yourself comes understanding others. Autoethnography provides an avenue for doing something meaningful for yourself and the world.'

This excerpt epitomises the conversations that autoethnographers will have with the uninitiated; the idea that writing about oneself must be easy. In her emotional response to the student, Carolyn highlights the tensions that have to be dealt with from the revelations of personal pain, the inclusion of other family members and the ability to write well enough to carry it off. The paper goes on to talk of the therapeutic value of writing, the partial and fragmented nature of capturing stories about the past and the ethics of including others.

ANALYTICAL AUTOETHNOGRAPHY

The current discourse of autoethnography refers almost exclusively to evocative autoethnography. In response to the growing success of evocative autoethnographic texts, Anderson (2006) is concerned that one of the unintended consequences is that other visions of what autoethnography can be will be obscured. Analytic auto-ethnography refers to

ethnographic work in which the researcher is (1) a full member in the research group or setting, (2) visible as such a member in the researcher's published texts, and (3) committed to an analytic research agenda focused on improving theoretical understandings of broader social phenomena. (p. 375)

This view is further endorsed by Atkinson (2006, p. 403), who agrees that all ethnographic work implies a degree of personal engagement; but what should be guarded against is 'the implicit assumption that self transformation is the main outcome of such research processes'. Ellis and Bochner's (2006) response to Anderson's paper was to express their fear that he was trying to tame autoethnography. They say

Autoethnography shows struggle, passion, embodied life and the collaborative creation of sense-making in situations in which people have to cope with dire circumstances and loss of meaning … it needs the researcher to be vulnerable and intimate … it shouldn't be used as a vehicle to produce distanced theorising. (p. 433)

Sarah Wall weaves her own experience of international adoption into the social science literature that doesn't appear to echo her own experience. In this example of analytical autoethnography, she is not trying to evoke a response to her personal experience, but to contribute to the discourse on international adoption.

RE-THINKING MOTHERHOOD AND KINSHIP IN INTERNATIONAL ADOPTION (WALL [FORTHCOMING])

The story of international adoption is a dramatic one. International adoption as a way of creating a family is common enough for most people to be familiar with it, however, it also invites continued questioning, theorizing, and research about the creation and meaning of non-biological motherhood and kinship. Adoption continues to be a highly stigmatized mode of family formation, largely because of the way western society privileges biological kinship (Fisher, 2003). Adoptive kinship and motherhood are often judged according to the familiar, 'natural' model of biological reproduction (Brakman and Scholz, 2006). Understandings about biological motherhood seep into discussions about adoption, resulting in pervasive understandings of adoptive motherhood and kinship as second-rate and leading to over-determinations of the experience of adoptive motherhood (Brakman and Scholz, 2006). Flowing from this emphasis on biological relatedness, the story of international adoption all too easily becomes one about otherness, disruption, and risk. In this chapter, I consider my own experience as the mother of an internationally adopted child as a way to challenge idealistic and stereotypical notions of motherhood and adoption and re-think the meaning and nature of non-biological kinship.

For twelve years, I have been the mother of a son, now 14 years old, adopted from Romania. (My husband of 21 years and my two biological daughters are also part of my family and this story.) While academic analyses of adoption, as presented in the literature, are not always part of awareness in ordinary life, I have, as an academic as well as a parent, ventured into the literature in order to analyze my experience sociologically ...

She concludes:

Extending Theory on Adoptive Kinship

Although adoption is commonplace, it has received remarkably little attention from social scientists and very little critical examination of negative societal assumptions about adoption has occurred (Fisher, 2003). Several adoptive mothers who are also academics have started to open the door to deeper questioning of the grand and pervasive societal discourses about adoption. I add my voice to theirs to challenge the 'bias toward biological reproduction and [the way] this bias infiltrates the language and experience of adoptive mothers' (Brakman and Scholz, 55). For me this bias impacted my decision to adopt and the kind of adoption I would pursue, my approach to negotiating issues of race and culture, and my experiences with both the process of adoption itself and with ongoing family life.

I love my son. My connection to him is not genetic but it is fully embodied. As with my biological children, I have experienced fatigue in caring for him, a visceral sense of worry during hard times, a swelling of my heart when I am proud of him, and a feeling that part of me is missing when I am away from him. That my connection to him should be seen as anything but natural distresses me, yet I am edified by Howell's description of kinship that is constituted apart from biogenetic procreation: By eating the same food over time, sharing emotional states, being in close physical proximity to people and objects, and being part of the shared creation of a family's destiny, a child becomes one's own, not just legally but *physically* (467). This is a new and productive way for our society to think about kinship and a helpful way of explaining kinship as I have experienced it. The pursuit of new theories about kinship in adoptive families is a potentially huge opportunity for sociologists and I am inspired by my own experience to consider these questions further.

While in communication with Sarah over the inclusion of her extract in this chapter, I note with interest the changes that she has been asked to make as a result of the review process. I note her comment, 'It's interesting how a personal story becomes shaped by other people as it goes along!' and reflect on the impact of others in the process of telling a personal story.

PERFORMATIVE AUTOETHNOGRAPHY

In contrast, Pelias (1999, p. ix) suggests that 'performance is a way of knowing ... and such knowing resides in the ontological and is perhaps best expressed in the poetic' which is an interesting contrast to the ideas of Bakhtin expressed earlier. He provides an extensive list of definitions of what performance is, of which the following is a small selection:

Performance is: a way of giving shape to haunting spirits, putting into form what disturbs, what fascinates, what demands attention; that is, performance is a way of formulating the unforgettable so that it might be forgotten.

Performance is: an act of becoming, a strategy for discovering oneself by trying on scripts to test their fit, a means of clothing oneself in various languages until one believes what one says.

Performance is: an aesthetic encounter, a seductive coalescence that catches you in time, a luscious lure that pulls you in close and pushes you away, over and over, as you lean forward, engaged and giddy, on the top of a sparkle of light. (Pelias, 1999, pp. 109, 111)

Denzin (2003, p. 258) goes further and suggests that 'performance ethnography is more than a tool of liberation. It is a way of being moral and political in the world ... (it) is a moral discourse'.

PERFORMING HISTORICAL NARRATIVE

I first encountered Amy Pinney's remarkable performance in a presentation at the second International Congress on Qualitative Inquiry in Champaign-Urbana, USA, in 2006, but it is her performance at the third conference in 2007 that I have chosen to illustrate performance as a method of inquiry. Amy displayed an embodied performance based on her thesis recovering the life work of Anna Baright Curry (1854–1924) (Pinney, 2007a; Pinney, 2007b). Anna Baright Curry was the founder of the School of Elocution and Expression but became 'dismissed from our disciplinary history … written out through habit' (Pinney, 2007a, p. i). Pinney describes archival research as an embodied act in her attempts to recover and uncover the life of Baright Curry.

Pelias (1999, p. ix) writes of the difficulties of translating the art of the stage to the page, but as he says 'to accept that duplicating performance experience in essay form may be impossible is not, however, to succumb to silence'.

The following extract from Pinney's work is enhanced by the inclusion of stage directions (in parentheses) which should enable you to grasp its aesthetic power and engage with the performance-like aspects.

'Artistic Paradox' (Pinney, 2007a)

My third performance of Anna Baright Curry took place at the Third International Congress on Qualitative Inquiry in Champaign-Urbana. … I told the audience that I was going to perform just one essay, 'Artistic Paradox', and attend to just one performance consideration: Costume. That's all, just costume. I did this in an effort to discern for myself and for my audience how much impact on a text just one (in this case historically) embodied fact could matter. (Perched on the edge of the beige folding table at the front of the conference room, she holds Anna's text in her hands, and begins to read in a brash, confident, modern way. Think Kathleen Turner.)

'I have a word further to say of what may seem a paradox – the fact that the artist in depicting character or dramatic situations gives himself to the character, and at the same time reserves the conscious direction of himself and the ability to stand outside of himself and judge of what he is doing in its relation to his conception of what he ought to do. This fact is as true of other forms of dramatic work as of impersonation.'

What we know for sure is that in 1897, Anna Baright Curry, founder of the School of Elocution and Expression, was not lecturing while perched on the edge of a table.

(She hops up and continues.)

'All art is in the sphere of consciousness.'

(She delivers this line like 'Awwwwwwwllllll Art is in the Sphere of Con-Scious-Ness'. Her legs are planted and spread far beyond shoulder width apart as she swoops her hands to the floor and back up, thus inscribing a sphere in the air between the audience and the stage. She then holds her hands high above her head, holding the sphere.)

What we also know for sure, is that in 1897, Anna was definitely wearing a skirt.

(Quickly and sheepishly snap legs together. Arms still holding the sphere in the air.)

'The artist himself becomes a part of his own consciousness in his activities.'

(Throughout this section she is obviously hyper-aware of the immobility of her knees.)

'Dramatic instinct not only enables the artists to know himself and to know characters other than himself, but it makes it possible for him to realize in experience the relation of his own activities to himself.'

(Extends one arm in expansive gesture to indicate the 'own set of activities'.)

'and also the relation of the activities of other characters to themselves.'

(Extends other arm in expansive gesture to indicate the 'other' set of activities. Holds pose.)

According to a costumer friend of mine who specializes in women's dress at the turn of the century, in 1897, the sleeves of Anna's dress were built as such to allow her arms to raise

(Lowers arms completely)

this much.

(Raises arms slightly. Holds arms stiff and straight and pointed toward the floor.)

'Imaginative thinking is the means by which the artist identifies his own life with the lives of other characters; but in order to think, there must be a conscious volitional activity in the choice of ideas, and in order to act a character, there is a conscious volitional choice in the selection of the signs of life that manifest the character.

'In addition, her skirts were ...

(snap wrists so that hands are at a ninety degree angle to wrists) ...

voluminous'.

'The criterion of judgement lies in the conception of the character in the artist's mind.'

(She attempts in vain to point her fingers to her head to indicate 'mind.'

Resignedly lowers fingers back down.)

...

(Leaning forward still earnestly, and pointing as much as she can without moving her upper arms, but leaning forward nonetheless, still struggling but beginning to feel incremental success in conveying these words in this body)

'to a degree that he realizes them as his own,'

(increasingly successful)

What we know for sure, is that in 1897, Anna

'and allows them to find actual realization through his own life and through his own form.'

Was corseted.

(Snap up to attention. All measure of temporary success vanishes. Defeated.)

Corseted not in the 'S' curve of the Gibson Girls that would come a few years later, but in the stick–straight, stand up, tucked in, and thrusted up kind of corseted.

...

According to my costumer friend, Anna's collar came up to about here.

(Indicates, with chin, a slight thrust upward).

This collar assured that the line from the bottom of her spine to the top of her crown was uninterrupted, undisturbed by trifles like nods and bends and sidelong glances. The collar also dictated the necessarily efficient use of a very clear, if compressed, airway from her lungs to her tongue.

...

Though these costumed constraints are new to me, they were not new to Anna. She was born into them: sleeves, corsets, skirts, collars and all. I've a feeling she manipulated then with a facility I lack. These constraints don't belong to me. They are hers. And she owned them.

... this performance, I battled what I felt to be Anna's emotional constraint that comes with such costuming. It turned out to be both hers and my own. Whalebone and fabric contain her. The fabric of her being contains me. I feel her as a squeeze. In the third performance, I learned that with or without 'accessories,' when I am in her body, it's harder to breath. She fits me like a corset.

PHENOMENOLOGY

As an academic supervisor of students doing masters degrees, I watch with interest as they grapple with ontological, methodological and epistemological considerations. Nowhere is this struggle more evident than in the tortuous angst that is precipitated by an entry into the world of phenomenology (Muncey, 2004). Phenomenology is a philosophical orientation adapted by social scientists to promote an understanding between individual states of consciousness, and social life which has undergone considerable reinterpretation and representation as it is adopted by different disciplines. My unease with phenomenology rests on two levels: (1) whether in fact the researcher is actually doing phenomenology and not some sociological interpretivist equivalent; and (2) whether overall the journey into the vagaries of Husserl versus Heidegger is worth it. I agree with Porter (2008, p. 268) that it is 'possible to jettison the baroque intricacies of high phenomenology and just use its simple basic assumptions, without any significant compromise to the integrity of research'.

It could be argued that all research has a philosophical basis but it is only those accused of muddle-headed anecdotalism at the qualitative end of the spectrum that are ever asked to justify this position in detail in every study. The simple-minded rationalists of course are rarely asked to justify the Popperian nature of their work. The scientific empiricism on which RCT is based is founded in the Age of Enlightenment. In this postmodern world of multiple realities, the certainties of Newtonian physics no longer exist and neither does the pursuit of the 'truth' about the body, so ably dissected by Descartes into body and mind.

My concern is really paramount when the students get to describing the phenomena they wish to investigate. It always necessitates asking, usually in in-depth interviews, about the 'lived experience' of the phenomena. At this point the student can be trapped by the difference between meaning of an experience and meaning in an experience. One is a philosophical question faithful to the tradition spawned by Husserl, the other can be gained by any type of social enquiry.

Take, for example the difference between the meaning **of** life and finding meaning **in** life. Short of life being described as 42 by Ford Prefect in the *Hitchhiker's Guide to the Galaxy* (Adams, 2002), such deep and meaningful considerations are avoided by most people. As I describe in my story in Chapter 2, we either take on the simple truth that God is the provider of life and all its sacred rituals, or, at the other extreme, in 'His' or 'Her' absence, like the existentialist Camus, we liken it to rolling a stone up hill only to find it rolling down again with monotonous regularity, as in the myth of Sisyphus (Camus, 2000). Most people do not engage in a philosophical quest about the meaning of their life; on a day-to-day basis they try to make meaning out of the experiences they have.

Telling the truth is also a philosophical stance and I suspect most everyday people engaging in research studies do not stop and consider this. All qualitative research requires the telling of a story from which meaningful data can be obtained. If phenomenology is so concerned about the lived experience of the participant, why are so many phenomenological analyses reduced to themes that combine to share experiences or commonalities? If a truly individual narrative is required, why not use narrative enquiry techniques and leave out the philosophising?

One student does appear to arrive at this conclusion after a very long journey, but it is arguable she found out more about herself than she did about teamworking.

In some respects what has evolved through the findings of this research journey would seem less to be about team working and rather more about the very essence of what it means to be human. The power within this research method is that of hearing the voices of those embraced within the phenomenon of study. Indeed a hermeneutic approach that holds the participant as the expert from whom we can all learn, has proved a valuable way towards understanding the complexities of such human encounters as teamwork. Yet perhaps it is the endless journey of circles within circles, the continual interpretation and understanding that never completes that is most appealing. For myself, such a method has been very much about enacting what we value as individuals, taking from what we discover, that which is most familiar and that we hold most dear but at the same time remaining open to the commitment of others. Perhaps in conclusion one could suggest that hermeneutic research is very much about a way of life. (Chappell, 2000)

For further discussion on the problems with phenomenology I refer you to Paley (1998), who presents a critique of the uses and abuses of phenomenology; or to Avis (2003) for a consideration of the whole methodological justification minefield. On the other hand, Max van Manen (2002) provides an excellent resource for the budding phenomenologist at Phenomenology on line.

NARRATIVE

Another method that overlaps and interweaves with autoethnography is narrative inquiry. People are natural storytellers; their stories give coherence and continuity to their existence (Lieblich et al., 1988). Polkinghorne (1998) goes further, arguing that narratives *are* peoples' identities; the stories people tell shape and construct the narrator's personality and reality as the story is retold and reconstructed throughout that individual's life.

Narrative inquiry gives insight into the narrator's systems of meaning, framed by their culture and social world (Lieblich et al., 1988). Phillips (1994, p. 14), in tracing the history of narrative enquiry, suggests that it is 'marked by the gradual erosion of the positivist model of man'. (Hones, 1998, p. 226) argues that narrative research moves 'one step further from the hermeneutic circle', which he suggests is the goal of interpretive social science.

Within the postmodern debate surrounding narrative research, much of the discussion appears to focus on contextualisation; whether the narrative *text* itself is different from the *context* or conditions of construction. Polkinghorne (1998) argues that the recorded narrative is a snapshot in time; the story changes according to the context in which it is told.

Mishler (1986), a pioneer of the use of narratives in research, regards this particular approach as a principle means of making sense of an experience.

Although the terms 'storytelling' and 'narrative' are often used synonymously, Wiltshire (1995) suggests making a distinction between the two. Frid et al. (2000, p. 695) describe a narrative as a version of events personally experienced by the narrator, while storytelling is 'the repeated telling or reading of a story by persons other than the narrator'. However, it remains a hotly contested area. Denzin (1989, p. 37) defines the narrative as 'a story that tells a sequence of events that are significant for the narrator and his or her audience'.

The argument that narratives need not be true to be relevant (Fredriksson and Lindstrom, 2002) is consistent with the idea of knowledge emerging from our subjective world view rather than induced from observation of the world. However, it must not be forgotten that on each occasion a story is told, its creation is based on the context in which it is being related (Frid et al., 2000). Nevertheless, while an individual may embellish or indeed fabricate the account of his experience, this does not discredit it for research purposes (Aranda and Street, 2001). They suggest that survey responses may also contain fabrications or embellishments but are nevertheless valued.

GENDERED STORIES

The diversity of feminist philosophy and methodology is acknowledged and celebrated. Indeed, feminist scholar Dale Spender states that at the core of all feminist ideas is the realisation that no single truth or authority or method can lead to the production of pure knowledge (Spender, 1985). Feminist critiques of positivism accuse this approach of rendering women's experiences as invisible as a consequence of the insistence on objectivity (Harding, 1987; Ussher, 1999). The philosopher Elizabeth Minnich (1982, p. 7) goes further, describing the positivist view of man or 'androcentric thought' as a 'devastating conceptual error'.

Drawing on the work of Michel Foucault, feminist scholars have moved away from the grand narratives of modernism towards a postmodern perspective (Davis and Fisher, 1993). Thus there is understanding and recognition that patriarchal oppression, rather than being monolithic and unidirectional, is in fact perpetuated through the dynamic interaction between women and the social constraints that structure their lives.

Michel Foucault (1980, pp. 81–4) coined the term 'subjugated knowledges' to include all the local, regional, vernacular, naive knowledges at the bottom of the hierarchy – the low Other of science. These are the non-serious ways of knowing that dominant culture neglects, excludes, represses, or simply fails to recognise. Subjugated knowledges have been erased because they are illegible; they exist, by and large, as active bodies of meaning, outside of books, eluding the forces of inscription that would make them legible, and thereby legitimate, ways of knowing. They are lost arts and records of encounters with power (Gingrich-Philbrook, 2005). Buzard (2003) suggests that widespread critiques of anthropology and advocacy for situated knowledges have created an atmosphere highly favourable to the rise of an autoethnography, although he suggests that its use has so far been uneven and undertheorised.

Feminist theory emerges from and responds to the lives of women, and because it is grounded in women's lives and seeks to discover the role and meaning of gender in those lives and within society, the personal narratives of women are essential primary sources for feminist research (Reinharz, 1992).

In discussing the representation of data in reflexive research reports, Freshwater and Rolfe (2004, p. 7) emphasise that 'there is no single authoritative reading of any text'; rather, the report should be 'open to deconstruction and multiple readings'. I would argue, in common with Ellis (1997), that the emotional engagement of the reader has a place within these multiple readings. As Benjamin (1968, p. 87) states 'the storyteller takes what she tells from experience – her own or that reported by others. And she in turn makes it the experience of those who are listening to her tale'.

A GENDERED STORY

Kitrina's story below incorporates the principles of narrative research in an autoeth-nographic way, embodying issues of gender and power in women's golf. Kitrina wrote this story based on her own experiences as a professional golfer, her life history research with women professional golfers, as well as on what she has seen commentating for the BBC at golf events.

The Pro-Am (Douglas and Carless, 2008)

One fine day…

A huge solid oak desk dominates the opulent office of Bernard Brasco, a tall large framed man in his early fifties. But long before anyone gets inside the office to take a look at the palatial setting, visitors are reminded that this is no ordinary office. The sign on the door, embossed lettering on a gold plaque, reads 'Chairman', as if anyone wouldn't know. Anyone who makes it this far inside Brasco HQ, a Jacobean manner house once inhabited by the Duke of Argyle, knows this is Bernard 'Brandsco' – the world recognised brand man.

The surroundings of his office testify not only his position within the business world but perhaps more tellingly his interest in sport – photographs on the walls and memorabilia alongside cricket, football, and golf trophies in a hand crafted oak cabinet, incidentally carved from trees on his own estate. In this holy of holies, the photographs anchor Bernard and illustrate what is important in his life, his religious heritage and proof of his standing in the world of sport. These photographs verify that he has played with the best in sport – not just watched them. They testify that these famous, courageous national heroes *know* Bernard and that they are his friends; they must be because there is a personal handwritten message on each one.

At the start of the gallery a small framed photo is illuminated by a single halogen spot light turning the man in running shorts into a three dimensional figure, his shiny wet skin is alive and tanned, his running vest limp, his face lined, he holds aloft a yellow coloured medal with a red and blue ribbon. Scrawled diagonally across the photo in bold felt tip pen are the words: 'Thanks for everything Bernard, xxx Seb.' Next to this is a larger framed photo with a picture light illuminating it from above showing Bernard and England's cricket captain, both dressed in crisply pressed white trousers with an impeccable crease running down the front and starched-like white shirts. Bernard's left arm is chummily around the man's shoulder and both hold bats under their right arms. Neatly written in biro the text reads: 'Bernard, next catch is yours! Ho ho!!! Mike.' And so the gallery goes on and on around the room until finally four men, one of them Bernard, stand in front of a tennis net, all holding rackets, bodies wet from the game, smiling faces, and the message in curly handwriting reads 'Bernard, next time you go to the net leave some for me – Andre.'

Today Bernard sits erect on the edge of a large leather armchair, planning his marketing budget for the coming year. His chief marketing executive Paul is with him looking at figures.

'Well the men's tour want a million next year' Paul says. 'I think that's excessive, it's too big a jump for us. But we can get the women a lot cheaper. Their prize funds start at a hundred thousand. I spoke with their CEO last week he said we could have a thirty team pro-am instead of just ten that we were offered from the men's tour.' Bernard looked at the figures disparagingly.

'Women's golf?' he queried in a condescending tone. 'Aren't they a load of butch dykes?'

'No, no Bernie,' Paul responded, with well practiced [sic] respect, shaking his head gently. 'Well that Nora Harding might be. But listen, I played in a couple of their pro-ams last year, these girls are really good. Here, look.' It was the media guide to the Ladies Tour. It covered the tournaments, the players, their earnings and their mug-shots. Bernard took the book and began to leaf through, his eyes drawn to the pictures.

'Well she looks very dodgy to me Paul!' Bernard grinned as he pointed to one player's black and white head and shoulder photo before he began to read the player's profile.

Five days later...

On the first tee arrive Bernard, Paul and an invited friend Ken. They are greeted by a tall Italian woman, her black hair tied in a pig-tail which cascades down her back, swishing like a pony's tail to and fro across the exposed tanned skin of her lower back, her tight pants accentuating her slender legs.

'Gentlemen,' says the starter, 'this is Monica Taresta, your professional for the day.'
In perfect English spoken with an evocative Italian accent, and an outstretched hand, Monica greets the trio. 'A pleasure to meet you. I am Monica.'

Bernard, asserting his position, immediately pushes forward with an outstretched body and pulls the young woman toward him, groping around her cheek in an effort to plant a kiss. It's a hot day and Bernard is sweaty, his watery grip is no more appealing than the slobbery peck on her cheek, but this is nothing new for Monica. The other two men are less pushy. Paul with an insecure step forward holds out his hand, Monica gently responds and nods her head. Finally Ken, awaiting his turn, shakes Monica's hand a little too enthusiastically – he is fixed by her dark eyes and clear complexion, he forgets to let go, she gently prizes her hand away from his grip.

'What balls have you got?' she asks.
'Would you like to inspect my balls?' Bernard asks, raising his eyebrows and giving a little chuckle.
'No, just tell me the make and number Bernard.' Monica responds.

Each member of the team needs to number their ball differently so that, should they be hit into a similar position, there is no confusion or breaking of the rules. Ball check complete it's safe to proceed. But, of course, every week, in every pro-am, some men always like to talk about their balls, compare them, laugh about them ...

...

The strike of the ball brings Bernard back to the present. Her ball is launched down the fairway. Bernard is amazed. How could this slip of a girl do that? Paul, less surprised but no less impressed, relishes the moment. Ken is in awe. Bernard is unable to disguise his momentary surprise. The flight of the ball, the power, the distance – nothing like the 'ladies' at his club. He didn't know women could hit the ball like that – not if they looked like *that* – his eyes momentarily drawn to the cleavage forming before him as Monica bends down to retrieve her tee peg.

Bernard is an average golfer. He believes, in his dreams, that he is a great golfer. If he'd wanted to be a pro he could have been. But he decided there was more power in business.

'On the tee Bernard Brasco!'

The starter announces – but it's too soon. Bernard suddenly realises a crowd has gathered, some spectators there to see Monica, the next group have arrived, a few other professionals have come onto the tee to talk with his pro. He looks at her ball, positioned in the middle of the fairway a long, long way away, and realises he must hit it further than this girl.

A bead of sweat forms on Bernard's brow, gaining weight and size before dripping onto the shaky grip he has taken on the club. He stands in the hitting position over the ball. His muscles look tense, his stance too wide, he swings too quickly – it's over in a flash. A huge divot flies up in the air and the ball squirts off into some bushes fifty yards away. Bernard does not look up. He ignores this all-too-public display of incompetence.

'Nice one Jessie!' shouts a voice from the crowd. 'Tell me old man does your husband play? I think you forgot your makeup and yellow handbag old boy!' Paul recognises the voice and nods toward Julian, a slightly inebriated client of Brandsco's. Bernard regains his poise:
'It's this Italian Julian – she's got me in a fluster!' Bernard shouts back without looking.
'Oooh! Now I see why you hit in the bushes! Maybe she'll help you look for it!' Julian sniggers.

Monica smiles, she's heard it all before. The groping, the bushes, the balls, the innuendos, they are not new, they are tiresome. But she smiles and nods her head graciously. In four hours the prostitution will be over. She leans back and allows it all to take place without becoming involved.

'On the tee representing Brandsco, Paul Goodfellow!' Paul is announced on the tee, his nervousness obvious to all, but he takes an iron out of the bag.
'Good idea.' Monica offers reassuringly when she sees that the easier to hit club has been preferred to the difficult, showy driver.

Paul makes a poor swing, his lack of confidence on the golf tee out of place, unlike his demeanour at work where he is confident, secure and at ease. Golf makes him look disorganised. The ball is hit from the toe of the club and makes a thin sound travelling only 120 yards or so down the fairway.

'That's OK there Paul.' Monica again reassures.

Ken is announced. He is more nervous than his associates, he can't balance the ball on the tee, his hands won't fit the grip, he can't remember how to swing, its all over in a hurried rush, the ball dispatched out of bounds.

'Better hit another,' Monica suggests. 'Don't worry, it is a better ball, only need two of us to score and Paul is down the middle.' Ken hunts in his bag for another ball, the crowd grow impatient. Eventually he finds a ball and scurries to the teeing area, his ability to balance the ball no better the second time round.
'Ken!' Monica calls, 'There is no hurry! Take your time, shorter swing, and no trying to hit it too hard this time.' She looks straight into his eyes, her warm stare and friendly smile drown her words. Ken makes a swipe, somehow hits the ball and sends it a few yards down into the right rough.

The team are off.

If postmodernism has taught us anything it's that there's a thin line between fact and fiction. We are taught to doubt history, question the narratives on which our culture is based and accept rewritings as just another perspective on 'the truth' The autoethnographer will occasionally be asked 'What is the difference between autoethnography and autobiography?' My first cynical response is that if you could make money out of publishing your story you would probably write it as an autobiography. However, these are usually portrayals of celebrated lives, the rich, famous and infamous.

THE MISERY MEMOIR GENRE

Before completing a chapter exploring where autoethnography fits with other qualitative approaches portraying personal experience, it is important to point out one very contemporary genre of writing that does not meet the criteria for auto-ethnographic research. This is the misery memoir genre, which appears to have a firm grip on culture. As much as 30% of the non-fiction paperback chart on any given week is made up of accounts of grinding childhood misery. At Harper Non-fiction, the leading publisher in the genre, these books are known as 'Inspirational Memoirs'. Waterstone's displays them together on a shelf labelled 'Painful Lives'. But within the publishing industry, the genre is referred to as 'misery lit'. Most observers trace the birth of misery literature to 2000 and Dave Pelzer's memoir, *A Child Called It* (Pelzer, 2000). In it, the American writer details the story of his outrageously cruel childhood at the hands of his alcoholic mother, although a happy ending is key to a successful memoir of this kind. In a publishing world dominated by misery memoirs, where the more grotesquely cruel the childhood, the bigger is the advance.

Just why they are so popular draws on an age old Aristotelian concept of catharsis – a requirement for purging pity and terror in a successful tragedy. Maybe there is more than just morbid fascination. Maybe this kind of voyeurism is seen to flatter readers' sense of moral outrage; and as 85% of misery lit, bought at supermarkets, is read by women, maybe they identify with the stories and find a great relief that one's lot isn't so bad (Addley, 2007).

The line between misery memoirs and autoethnography grows even thinner in the light of recent revelations about Margaret Seltzer's *Love and Consequences* (Jones, 2008). Presented as the memoir of a mixed-race drugs runner from South Central LA, it was revealed, just a week after the book's publication, that the entire story was fabricated. Margaret B. Jones, whose real name is Margaret Selzer, is all white and grew up in a well-to-do area of the city. She justified her actions as her 'opportunity to put a voice to people who people don't listen to' (Eastwood, 2008). Put like that, it sounds like autoethnography, but because it was a flagrant attempt to deceive and make money, it could be said to be exploiting the very people whose voice it attempts to speak for.

CONTEXTUAL RESEARCHER

At the end of this chapter, in positioning autoethnography as a methodology and a method, I suppose I need to reposition myself in the research world, lest this text should forever identify me with one approach. I am fascincated not only by the mixing of art and science that autoethnography attempts to do, but mixing science and social science as well as Mixed Methods that attempt to unite qualitative and quantitative approaches in imaginative ways. While I was bemoaning my inconstancy with a single research approach in the office one day, my colleague John Lees suggested that I think of myself as a contextually sensitive researcher, and this fitted me very well. The one thing that unites my eclectic range of research approaches is that the research question should direct the method by which the study is carried out. No single method fits all, and autoethnography is no exception.

Summary

- Social science researchers think they know something about society worth telling to others.
- All research that involves people is messy.
- Positioning oneself in the genre should include a consideration of the thinking in the field.

- Definitions of autoethnography question among many other things the idea of multiple layers of consciousness, the vulnerable self, the coherent self, critiquing the self in social contexts, subversion of dominant discourses and evocative potential.
- Bakhtin can provide a satisfactory philosophy for uniting art and science in a human science.
- Autoethnographers are broadly divided between two poles: those of analytical or evocative autoethnography.
- Autoethnography distances itself from the misery memoir.

FURTHER READING

Ellis, C. (1997) Evocative Autoethnography: Writing emotionally about our lives. In W. Tierney and Y.S. Lincoln (Eds) *Representation and the Text: Reframing the narrative voice.* SUNY, Albany, NY.

Carolyn Ellis provides more detail about what is in entailed in writing evocatively about our lives.

Spry, T. (2001) Performing autoethnography: An embodied methodological praxis. *Qualitative Inquiry,* **7**(6), 706–32.

Tami Spry offers evaluative standards for the autoethnographic performance, and draws attention to how we interpret culture through our self reflections.

REFERENCES

Adams, D. (2002) *The Hitchhiker's Guide to the Galaxy.* Picador, London.

Addley, E. (2007) So bad it's good. *The Guardian,* 15 June, p. 4.

Anderson, L. (2006) Analytic autoethnography. *Journal of Contemporary Ethnography,* **35**(4), 373–95.

Aranda, S. and Street, A. (2001) From individual to group: Use of narratives in a participatory research process. *Journal of Advanced Nursing,* **33**(6), 791–7.

Atkinson, P. (2006) Rescuing autoethnography. *Journal of Contemporary Ethnography,* **35**(4), 400–4.

Avis, M. (2003) Pearls, pith and provocation. Do we need methodological theory to do qualitative research? *Qualitative Health Research,* **13**(7), 995–1004.

Bakhtin, M.M. (Ed.) (1981) *The Dialogic Imagination: Four essays.* University of Texas Press, Austin, TX.

Barone, T. (2008) How Arts-based Research Can Change Minds. In M. Cahnmann-Taylor and R. Siegesmund, *Arts-based Research in Education: Foundations for practice.* Routledge, New York, pp. 28–49.

Barone, T. and Eisner, E. (2006) Arts-based Educational Research. In J. Green, G. Camili and P. Elmore, *Complementary Methods for Research in Education*. American Educational Research Association, Washington, DC.

Bayard, P. (2008) *How to Talk about Books You Haven't Read*. Granta Books, London.

Becker, H. (1986) *Doing Things Together*. North Western University Press, Evanston, IL.

Benjamin, W. (1968) *Illustrations*. Harcourt, Brace and World, New York.

Boje, D.M. (1991) The storytelling organization: A study of story performance in an office supply firm. *Administrative Science Quarterly, 36*, 106–26.

Borbasi, S. (1994) Insider ethnography. *Nursing Inquiry, 1*, 57.

Brakman, S-V. and Scholz, S.J. (2006) Adoption, ART and a re-conception of the maternal body: Toward embodied maternity. *Hypatia, 21*(1), 54–73.

Buzard, J. (2003) On auto-ethnographic authority. *Yale Journal of Criticism, 16*, 61–91.

Camus, A. (2000) *The Myth of Sisyphus*. Penguin, Harmondsworth.

Chappell, P. (2000) *Teamwork: Myth or Reality? A phenomenological inquiry to explore the reality of teamwork within the primary health care role*. University of Cambridge, Cambridge.

Davis, K. and Fisher, S. (Eds) (1993) *Negotiating at the Margins: The gendered discourses of power and resistance*. Rutgers University Press, New Brunswick, NJ.

Denzin, N.K. (1989) *Interpretive Interactionism*. Sage, Thousand Oaks, CA.

Denzin, N.K. (1992a) The Many Faces of Emotionality. In C. Ellis, *Investigating Subjectivity: Research on lived experience*. Sage, London, pp. 17–30.

Denzin, N.K. (1992b) *Symbolic Interactionism and Cultural Studies*. Blackwell, Cambridge, MA.

Denzin, N.K. (2003) *Performance Ethnography. Critical pedagogy and the politics of culture*. Sage, Thousand Oaks, CA.

Douglas, K. and Carless, D. (2008) The team are off: Getting inside women's experiences in professional sport. *The Journal of Sport Literature, XXV*(1), 241–51.

Eastwood, J. (2008) End of the line for misery memoirs? *Arts Hub*. Retrieved November 2008, from http://www.artshub.co.uk/uk/news.asp?sc=&sId=171493&sType=column

Economic and Social Research Council (ESRC) (2008) What is social science? Retrieved 24 October 2008, from http://www.esrc.ac.uk/ESRCInfoCentre/what_is_soc_sci/.

Ellis, C. (1997) Evocative Autoethnography: Writing emotionally about our lives. In W. Tierney and Y. S. Lincoln, *Representation and the Text: Reframing the narrative voice*. SUNY, Albany, NY.

Ellis, C. (1999) He*art*ful autoethnography. *Qualitative Health Research, 9*(5), 669–83.

Ellis, C. and Bochner, A. (2000) Autoethnography, Personal Narrative, Reflexivity: Researcher as subject. In N. Denzin and Y. Lincoln, *The Handbook of Qualitative Research*. Sage, Newbury Park, CA, pp. 733–68.

Ellis, C.S. and Bochner, A.P. (2006) Analyzing analytic autoethnography – an autopsy. *Journal of Contemporary Ethnography, 35*(4), 429–49.

Fisher, A.P. (2003) Still not quite as good as having your own: Toward a sociology of adoption. *Annual Review of Sociology, 29*, 335–361.

Foucault, M. (1980) *Power/Knowledge: Selected interviews and other writings 1972–77*. Pantheon, New York.

Fredriksson, L. and Lindstrom, U. (2002) Caring conversations – psychiatric patients' narratives about suffering. *Journal of Advanced Nursing, 40*(4), 396–404.

Freshwater, D. and Rolfe, G. (2004) *Deconstructing Evidence-based Practice*. Routledge, London.

Frid, I., Ahlen, J., Bergbom, I. (2000) On the use of narratives in nursing research. *Journal of Advanced Nursing, 32*(3), 695–703.

Gardiner, M. and Bell, M.M. (1998) Bakhtin and the Human Sciences: A brief introduction. In *Bakhtin and the Human Sciences*. Sage, London, Ch. 1.

Gee, J.P. (1992) *The Social Mind: Language, ideology, and social practice.* Bergin and Garvey, New York.

Gergen, K.J. (1995) *Construction, Critique, and Community.* Harvard University Press, Cambridge, MA.

Gingrich-Philbrook, C. (2005) Autoethnography's family values: Easy access to compulsory experiences. *Text and Peformance Quarterly*, **25**(4), 297–314.

Gray, R. (2000) The use of research-based theatre in a project related to metastatic breast cancer. *Health Expectations*, **3**, 137–44.

Halling, S. (2002) Making phenomenology accessible to a wide audience. *Journal of Phenomenological Psychology*, **33**(1), 19–38.

Harding, S. (1987) Is there a Feminist Method? In *Feminism and Methodology: Social Science Issues.* Indiana University, Bloomington, IN; Open University Press, Buckingham.

Hayano, D. (1979) Auto-ethnography: Paradigms, problems, and prospects. *Human Organisation*, **38**(1), 99–104.

Holquist, M. (2002) *Dialogism.* Routledge, London.

Hones, D.F. (1998) Known in part: The transformational power of narrative inquiry. *Qualitative Inquiry*, **4**(2), 225–48.

Jones, K. (2006) A biographic researcher in pursuit of an aesthetic: The use of arts-based (re)presentations in 'performative' dissemination of life stories. *Qualitative Sociological Review*, **11**(1), 66–85.

Jones, M.B. (2008) *Love and Consequences: A Memoir of hope and survival.* Riverhead Books, New York.

Langellier, K. (1999) Personal narrative, performance, performativity: Two or three things I know for sure. *Text and Peformance Quarterly*, **19**, 125–44.

Law, J. (2003) Making a mess with method. Retrieved 5 September 2008, from http://www.lancs.ac.uk/fass/sociology//papers/law-making-a-mess-with-method.pdf

Lieblich, A., Tuval, L., Mashiach, R., Zilbert, T. (1988) *Narrative Research.* Sage Publications, New York.

Minnich, E. (1982) A devastating conceptual error: How can we not be feminist scholars? *Change* (April), 7–9.

Mishler, E. (1986) *Research Interviewing: Context and narrative.* Harvard University Press, Cambridge, MA.

Mishler, E.G. (1984) *The Discourse of Medicine. Dialectics of medical interviews.* Ablex, Norwood, NJ.

Muncey, T. (2004). 'Is the philosophical angst of phenomenology really worth the effort?' paper presented at the Advances in Qualitative Methods Conference, University of Alberta, Edmonton, Canada, January.

Muncey, T. (2009) Does Mixed Methods Constitute a Change in Paradigm? In S. Andrews and L. Halcomb, *Mixed Methods Research for Nursing and the Health Sciences.* Blackwell Publishing, Oxford, Ch. 2.

Muncey, T. and Robinson, R. (2007) Extinguishing the voices: Living with the ghost of the disenfranchised. *Journal of Psychiatric and Mental Health Nursing*, **14**, 79–84.

Neisser, U. (1976) *Cognition and Reality.* Freeman, San Francisco, CA.

Paley, J. (1998) Misinterpretive phenomenology: Heidegger, ontology and nursing research. *Journal of Advanced Nursing*, **27**(4), 817–24.

Pelias, R. (1999) *Writing Performance: Poeticizing the researcher's body.* Southern Illinois University Press, Carbondale and Edwardsville, IL.

Pelzer, D. (2000) *A Child Called It.* Topeka Bindery, Topeka, KS.

Phillips, D.C. (1994) Telling it straight – issues in assessing narrative research. *Educational Psychologist*, **29**(1), 13–21.

Pinney, A. (2007a) 'Archiving Anna Baright Curry: Performances of evidence and eviden-tiary performances. Speech communication.' Unpublished PhD thesis, Carbondale, Southern Illinois University.

Pinney, A. (2007b) 'Performing historical evidence', paper presented at the Third Interna tional Congress of Qualitative Inquiry, University of Illinois, Urbana-Champaign, May.

Polkinghorne, D. (1998) *Narrative Knowing and the Human Sciences*. State University of New York Press, New York.

Polkinghorne, D. (2004) *Practice and the Human Sciences: The case for a judgement-based practice of care*. State University of New York Press, New York.

Porter, S. (2008) Nursing research and the cults of phenomenology. *Journal of Research in Nursing*, **13**(4), 267–8.

Proust, M. (2003) *In Search of Lost Time: The way by Swanns*. Penguin, Harmondsworth.

Rapport, F., Wainwright, P. and Elwyn, G. (2005) 'Of the edgelands': Broadening the scope of qualitative methodology. *Medical Humanities*, **31**(1), 37–43.

Reed-Danahay, D. (Ed.) (1997) *Auto/Ethnography: Rewriting the self and the social*. Berg, Oxford.

Reinharz, S. (1992) *Feminist Methods in Social Research*. Oxford University Press, Oxford.

Rhind, D. (2003) *Great Expectations: The social sciences in Britain*. Commission on the Social Sciences, London.

Rudge, T. (1996) Re-writing ethnography: The unsettling questions for nursing research raised by post-structural approaches to 'the field'. *Nursing Inquiry*, **3**, 146–52.

Spender, D. (1985) *For the Record: The meaning and making of feminist knowledge*. Women's Press, London.

Spry, T. (2001) Performing autoethnography: An embodied methodological praxis. *Qualitative Inquiry*, **7**(6), 706–32.

Stevenson, J. (2006) *Good Women*. Vintage, London.

Todres, L. (1998) The qualitative description of human experience: The aesthetic dimension. *Qualitative Health Research*, **8**(1), 121–7.

Todres, L. (2000) Writing phenomenological-psychological descriptions: An illustration attempting to balance texture and structure. *Auto/Biography*, **8**(1&2), 41–8.

Ussher, J.M. (1999) Feminist Approaches to Qualitative Health Research. In M. Murray and K. Chamberlain, *Qualitative Health Psychology*. Sage, London, Ch. 7.

Van Manen, M. (2002) Phenomenology on Line. Retrieved November 2008, from http://www.phenomenologyonline.com/

Wall, S. (forthcoming) Re-thinking Motherhood and Kinship in International Adoption. In F. Latchford, *Adoption and Mothering*. Demeter Press, Toronto.

Wiltshire, J. (1995) Telling a story, writing a narrative: Terminology in health care. *Nursing Inquiry*, **2**(2), 75–82.

4
PLANNING AN AUTOETHNOGRAPHIC ACCOUNT

CHAPTER PREVIEW

Writing strategies
Creativity
Artistic tools
Writing tactics
A sporting chance
The Journey
The Body
The garden
Windowsill of life
Technique to stimulate imagination
Windowsill of life revisited
Songs
Starting to write
Reflections on starting to write
Writing phases
Aids to successful writing
Who are we writing for?
Other writers on writing
Voice

At this point I hope you are starting to take on board the idea that your story is important and worth telling. You have seen how others have charted the seas that you want to sail on and you feel you have enough methodological support for your journey. You have lived vicariously through the voyages of discovery of some others, but now it is time to get started on your own expedition. What strategies can you employ to assist you in transforming your experience into a creation to set before an audience for their consideration?

WRITING STRATEGIES

Richardson (2001, p. 35) states that 'writing is a method of discovery, a way of finding out about yourself and your world'. It is intensely personal, takes lots of practice and continually evolves. If it is to be used to convey something of oneself to a stranger, then writing tactics are required to evoke the researcher's vulnerable self. This involves techniques for releasing creativity and stimulating the imagination. In this chapter, I suggest the use of the snapshot to describe both literary and pictorial episodes, the stimulus of artefacts to conjure up feelings and thoughts, and the use of metaphor to enable deeply personal experiences to be layered and disguised without losing meaning. Practical hints to enhance the creative process will supplement the craft of producing a finished piece of work, which will also consider ways of re-presenting work in more imaginative forms.

CREATIVITY

People are inherently creative beings; we possess imaginations that can take us on our own flights of fantasy and into shared imaginations with others. On a daily basis we struggle to make sense of others' actions around us and do this by drawing on the sum of our own experiences to date. We are all implicit psychologists trying to make sense of the world around us. Who hasn't sat in crowded places and pieced together the details of other people's behaviour and tried to make sense of it?

Bohm (2004, p. xv) suggests that

> the human being is in the unique position of perceiving the dynamism and movement of the world around him, while at the same time realising that the means by which this perception takes place – one's own mind – is of an equivalent order of creativity, participating intimately with the world which it observes.

It is our capacity for reflexivity, the awareness of being aware, that allows us to represent and re-present the products of our imaginations in a variety of ways. I would even go so far as to say we have a destiny to be creative. Unfortunately, we have a tendency to label our creative endeavours as hobbies and struggle to keep the serious world of work/research in an objective style.

When you look at the seedhead in picture 1, do you see a weed or a magical example of the potential for creating future flowers or an exquisite artistic arrangement? It is this transformation of thinking that turns a simple experience into an artistic creation. Creativity might be considered a necessary part of life (Cameron, 1995). If we don't seek to fulfil our potential, we might wither and die.

PICTURE 1   SEEDHEAD

Unfortunately, in our highly competitive society we tend to measure our success in terms of money earned or successful careers. We dismiss the many talents that we have, those that don't achieve these ends, as hobbies or time-wasting activities. Writing that flows from the heart can transform experience into a state of bliss. The state of bliss, which gives potential access to the numinous or the spiritual in our lives, is something of a mystery to most people. It is captured in those moments when time appears to stand still, when we feel in tune with and inseparable from the universe. Fleeting moments of joy or long periods of deep satisfaction affect us physically, emotionally and psychologically, but are really quite a spiritual phenomenon. It is difficult to find the secret to capturing this sensation in life. What do you do that appears to make time disappear, where you feel content, satisfied, fulfilled? The easiest place I find it is in the garden, particularly in the greenhouse on an early spring morning; or assembling patches of fabric into patchwork quilts in the depths of winter. Finding a style and a voice of your own, which silences the critics in your head, I believe is an important aspect of autoethnography. This style and voice might metamorphose into a poem or a picture, a story or a drama or a film, but it should allow the recipient of the piece, the reader or the viewer, access to the inner story that cannot be told by other more conventional means.

ARTISTIC TOOLS

I began to realise that artistic tools are far more helpful in portraying the physical feelings, thoughts and emotions that expose my vulnerable self (Muncey, 2000; Muncey, 2004; Muncey, 2005). In the next chapter, I will deal with issues that arise in writing about experiences that involve memory; suffice it to say here that memory is a central issue in personal recollections. Russell (1999, p. 275) suggests that 'fragmentary recollections which are rich in detail and are characterized by disjunctions require "writing tactics" to draw attention to these disjunctions so that personal history can be implicated in larger social formations and historical processes'. Writing tactics require attention to literary and poetic conventions so that these do not prevent the story being understood. The tactics that I will focus on are the use of snapshots, artefacts, poetry and metaphor. However, the benefit of using a writing tactic such as metaphor has led me into another controversy in the world of research. Stories using devices like metaphor are typically classified as art, and as such denied existence in the rational world of research.

WRITING TACTICS

While taking creative writing classes, two important mantras were impressed on me. First, 'writers are people who write' – not special people with hidden magical powers but people who take up a pen, or sit down at a keyboard, and write; arguably the rest is practice and having something to say. The second important refrain is 'don't explain and don't complain'. This means setting down the words or drawing the picture without a constant evaluator in your head. I have described mine as an incessant whine in my right ear with its constant railing and appeal to my insecurities. To remind myself to override this 'noise', I keep a model parrot who symbolises the positive feedback that is necessary to keep going. Mykhalovskiy (1996, p. 135) talks of how his 'writing freezes' as he attempts to write in a voice that doesn't fit his purpose, and I know I can find myself overwhelmed by the voices of others whose polished finished text mocks me and diminishes my confidence.

Snapshots

Wittgenstein (1953) thought of the relationship between truth and reality as the same as between a picture and what it represents; and pictures have come to play a significant part in the recounting of my story. I have become fascinated by snapshots that capture episodes of life like stills in a film; they convey the skeleton of a life without the flesh and consciousness of the being (Muncey, 2005).

Visual imagery can be a useful adjunct to autoethnographies but the selection of snapshots is not without its problems. To what extent do images portray a 'truth' beyond the written text and do you agree with Kompf (1999) that

> Life is not how it is or how it was, but rather how it is interpreted, reinterpreted, told and retold. It is the story of our lives that we narrate to ourselves in an episodic, sometimes semi-conscious, virtually uninterrupted monologue. A photo does not represent a vacation, a story about me does not represent me … they are memory teasers (Kompf, 1999, p. 12)

This idea of the memory teaser is evoked in a story called 'Thanks for the Memory' (Ahern, 2008, p. 107). Joyce has returned to her family home to stay with her father.

He puts the bags down by the hall's wall of photographs, there to provide any visitor who crosses the threshold with a crash course of the Conway family history. Dad as a boy, Mum as a girl, Dad and Mum courting, married, my christening, communion, debutant ball and wedding. Capture it frame it display it: Mum and Dad's school of thought. It is funny how people mark their lives, the benchmarks they choose to decide when a moment is more of a moment than any other. For life is made of them. I like to think the best ones of all are in my mind, that they run through my blood in their own memory bank for no one else but me to see.

This captures the phenomenon of the family snapshot, certain moments frozen in time, but I am always intrigued by the kinds of pictures that are captured. They tend to celebrate the happy memories of childhood and significant transitions, such as christenings and weddings; they rarely capture the funeral or the episode of illness, so even our snapshots are not without societal conventions.

Snapshots are both artefacts and metaphors, captured for a moment in time. Barthes (1981, p. 82) suggests that the photograph does not 'call up the past (nothing Proustian in a photograph). The effect it produces upon me is not to restore what has been abolished (by time, by distance) but to attest that what I see has indeed existed'. In a sixtieth of a second the camera can capture an image that will serve to add a visual dimension to a memory. For that split second the picture represents a truth but to what extent can this be trusted? I have one photograph of myself six weeks in to nurse training, in full uniform looking the epitome of the stereotypical nurse of the early 1970s. Historical now with the short skirt, crisp white apron and jaunty cap, but I am reminded in this photo of a very transitory moment in my life when I was without a fringe. In the photo for some reason now lost to me my hair sweeps back from my forehead and under my cap. Over the years my hairstyle has changed very slowly but the one constant has been the maintenance of a deep fringe. My identity relies upon this constant and yet in one brief period of my life there is an image that demonstrates that this has not always been the case.

I am further reminded of the idiosyncrasies of images by seasonal pictures of my garden. The exact same spot in winter and summer will reveal a completely different view of the scene; both present a truth but no one is more accurate or more evocative than the other. Images do not help in the transitory nature of memories but they can stimulate memory, as Kompf suggests.

Artefacts

While I accept that photographs are artefacts of a kind I am specifically alluding here to other products generally referred to as 'manufactured'. You are surrounded by artefacts that have degrees of significance in your life. As I sit at my desk my eye is immediately drawn to an empty mug. I'm instantly transported to the pottery near the ferry at Uig on the Isle of Skye, Scotland. I can hear the seagulls screeching and the blast of the ferry horn as I discover this exquisite pottery and watch the potters at work.

The books that surround me convey something of my eclectic interests. There are also many memories of holidays, family and students, so that it is a wonder I can focus to write. I'm also reminded of the power of clutter to cause energy to stagnate and caution the reader to consider the artefacts that surround them with great care (Kingston, 1996). However, all these artefacts can help to stimulate the imagination for writing about experience. Some have special significance, such as the glass paperweight given to me by a grateful patient, but the artefacts that creatively affect differing levels of experience are, I believe, the ones that connect to deep personal experiences.

When I was trying to convey my sense of powerlessness in a world that tried to deny my story, I was drawn to those artefacts that represented powerful agents (Muncey, 2005): the uniforms associated with various professional and academic groups; the school reports that at first praised my success and then later blighted my confidence with no real concern as to what had transformed the girl from one who was 'alert and lively, working diligently' to one who was 'making little effort, lacking concentration, had a most unpleasant attitude and showing serious signs of inattention'. The upside-down watch became a symbol of connection to a time and place that I never quite completely belonged to. I couldn't afford one to start with and later rejected it as a symbol of a repressive regimen that served to keep nurses subservient to doctors, a metaphor for all that I disliked about institutional care.

Poetry

Poetry is a form of language that can generate new ways of thinking. Bachelard (1994, p. 15) said that 'The great function of poetry is to give us back the situation of our dreams'. In *The Poetics of Space* he is describing our houses not only as the embodiment of home but the embodiment of dreams, a place where we daydream. He suggests that we all have a house of 'dream memory' where imagination and memory are united. Poetry perhaps serves best to make the 'familiar' in our lives 'unfamiliar' (Myerhoff, 1986); to trouble the unconscious into recognising new ways of looking at and reflecting on experience. Maltby (2003, p. 66) describes this as 'a complex coordination between both conscious and unconscious forms of thinking and feeling to create a new identity that moves beyond both'.

Speedy (2005, p. 287) introduces me to the idea of 'found poetry', a form of poetry that is co-constructed from words or phrases found in particular contexts. I am suggesting that the stimulus for 'found poetry' could come from the same artefacts that inspire thoughtful reflection.

Susanna Kaysen uses an interesting artefact as the stimulus for her recollections in *Girl Interrupted*. She describes the impact of Vermeer's painting *Girl Interrupted at her music* (Vermeer 1660–61) on her own life. She saw this image just before an experience, that preceded her plummetting descent into mental illness, interrupted her life with others and her expected way of life. In the same way that the girl in the painting yearns to leave her world, so too did Susanna Kaysen.

Interrupted at her music: as my life had been, interrupted in the music of being seventeen, as her life had been, snatched and fixed on canvas: ... one moment made to stand still and to stand for all the other moments, whatever they would be or might have been. She asks 'What life can recover from that?' (Kaysen, 2000, p. 167)

Fascinated by Kaysen's idea of interruption, I found the word 'arrested' kept reverberating in my mind. The interruption to my life of teenage pregnancy had involved arrests in all interpretations of the word and a further poetic iteration of my story materialised.

'Arrested at the Gates of Eden'

Arrested
Captured in an oppressive childhood
Isolated in a rural idyll
Neglected
Abused
Created a lifelong inability to play

Arrested
Plucked from loving arms
into the arms of the law.
Shamed
Named
Created a lifelong intolerance of injustice.

Arrested
Snatched from the jaws of childhood
Into the responsibilities of motherhood
Constrained
Tamed
Created a lifelong craving for clear boundaries

Arrested
by the beauty of life which emerges in the mysteries of the garden
made available for contemplation
Blooming
Imagining
I resurrect my capacity to create.

~

Metaphor

Traditional attitudes toward metaphor can be traced to the historical development of western science. Those most responsible for developing and interpreting science in the 17th and 18th centuries had an aversion to the use of figurative language. Metaphor was viewed largely as an element of grammar and style, not as a useful device for conveying meaning. The empiricist philosophers believed that metaphor could give rise only to confusion by obscuring the categorical distinctions between words. As I go on to discuss in the next chapter, Locke expressed the philosopher's mistrust of figurative language (Nidditch, 1975). This is in direct comparison to Derrida (1978), who said that all language is metaphorical.

Lakoff and Johnson (1980, p. 103) remind us that 'the concepts that govern our thought are not just matters of the intellect. They also govern our everyday functioning, down to the most mundane details'. They suggest that metaphors are the structures that guide our hidden assumptions, for example argument is so synonymous with war that we talk of winning and losing and going head to head, having a battle of wills, so that it is almost impossible to see an argument as a dance. Being caught up in a dance is a very useful metaphor for the entanglements that lead to difficulties in relationships. Many of the circular arguments in relationships are because the steps of the dance are so familiar that when our partner leads, we follow. The steps draw us backwards and forwards into the tango of frustration, with the same outcome predictable every time unless we learn not to get caught up in the dance. As with all metaphors, their usefulness is that they can be extended and changed to provide a different way of viewing the world. If arguments are a dance, then we can learn new steps or learn a new dance or change partners. If arguments are a war, the winning is important, going for the kill and counter-attacking, from which it is very difficult to back down. In my frustration at how teenage pregnancy, in western culture, is always seen as a form of moral decline, I wanted to try and change it to one of 'sporting chance'.

A SPORTING CHANCE

Now that the government has launched a criticism of the Child Support Agency (CSA), and the Countryside Alliance are seeking an injunction to stop the ban on fox hunting there is bound to be a re-emergence of these two topics in the media. One is the metaphorical hounding of men to support their biological offspring, and the other the literal hounding of foxes for sport. Top of the list for media attention is usually the teenage mother, whose contribution to the moral decline of society is only surpassed by the killing for sport of a small number of foxes. There aren't many occasions when fox hunting and teenage pregnancy would appear in the same article, although today they share much space in the current media. Both concern relatively small numbers of people and yet both are suggested to be contributing to the moral decline in our society. Where they differ is in their economic position and the strength of their public voice. They both involve victims, namely the young mother and her baby, and the fox; and both are subject to disagreements over the best way to deal with them. The baby that results from the sexual act of two young people is considered a 'problem', unlike the baby from, say, two 25-year-olds. Aborting this 'problem' appears only slightly more immoral than keeping it. Likewise, foxes are unwanted and are vermin to some, but hunting them is more immoral than destroying them in other ways.

(I then go on to elaborate on my perspective of the problem before concluding.)

The withholding of good quality housing, support and advice about relationships from teenage mothers, together with allowing them very little money, means that the real problems of teenage pregnancy are doomed to continue, however much research monies are spent on investigating them. Teenage pregnancy is only problematised by those who would seek to reduce the numbers. It is an interesting but odd harbinger of a society's decline; given that I've always been intrigued that the powerless, disenfranchised and poor teenage mother can be vilified as a contributor to any sort of decline, apart from her own. I would suggest that if the act of teenage pregnancy was distanced from concerns about finances and more focused on the psychological and emotional impact on the young woman and her baby, we would tackle the situation in a very different way.

This is why the rich and powerful fox hunting community is interesting. The fertility of foxes appears to be as much of a problem as that of young girls. Offering them contraceptive advice would be ludicrous. The baby, like the young fox, is a convenient decoy to occupy the minds of the general population who always want to blame problems in society on the voiceless minority. Young foxes are thought to need protection from those who would seek to use them for sport. Statistically, I suspect they are much more likely to die of hunger, road traffic accidents and predators. I don't hear concern for reducing these problems. If foxes could be given a voice, I suspect they wouldn't consider that death by hounds was of any greater significance than death from traffic. Their real concerns would probably be finding a home and feeding their young, with a sporting chance of survival in a rapidly changing society. As a teenage mum, I would posit the view that this is all I wanted to do as well until the 'experts' started to tell my story differently.

~

THE JOURNEY

Would the metaphor of a sporting chance work? We are a world obsessed by sport, so I can't see why not. I suppose it has a hint of winners and losers about it but at least there is always a goal to strive for, a sense of belonging to something worthwhile, and where there are rewards if you strive for them. However, isn't it really environmental awareness, and seeing the fox and the young mother in context?

A more common metaphor invoked in research is that of the journey. I am intrigued by this that many invoke to describe a period of discovery or a process of learning. The PhD, the process of counselling, the experience of bereavement – each may be evoked as a journey. However, not all journeys are the same, not all of them lead to new places or to new ways of thinking; some journeys are backwards and forwards over and over the same ground or round and round in circles, coming back to the same place unchanged and undifferentiated, not unlike the journey of millions of commuters every day. The difference between being a tourist and being a traveller springs to mind. A tourist sets out to a known, pre-planned destination, carefully controlled with all risk minimised, probably organised by a travel agent, and returns home with memories of the occasion but probably unchanged by the people or the culture of the destination. A traveller on the other hand sets out to explore, prepares an itinerary but relishes the experiences of interacting with the places that he/she pitches up in. However, commuting is also a journey. Going backwards and forwards so often between two places until eventually all the trips blur into one means that the commuter is forced to fill the void with other activities to relieve the boredom. Nothing new is learnt and the discourse among travellers will only be about the late train, or the disrupted service or the irritation of the noisy disruptive passenger.

I think a great deal of research is like the commuter's journey: a predictable shuffle between expected destinations, with safety and comfort the desired outcome but with no hint of adventure. Autoethnography could be likened to an adventure; setting off with a map and compass and some understanding of the territory but not hidebound by expectations or predictability.

Romanyshyn (1982) suggested that subjective experience is best thought of as a metaphorical reality. He suggests that the growth of science as a way of making sense of the world is marked by a change in the metaphors used to reflect reality.

THE BODY

Another common metaphor in our society is the body. We talk of a body of knowledge, the body politic or the body of the church, and one fairly precise definition of discourse is: 'A body of ideas, concepts and beliefs which become established as knowledge or as an accepted world view. These ideas become a powerful framework for understanding and action in social life' (Bilton et al., 1996, p. 657).

The medical model of the body is one such powerful discourse, where mind and body are separated into a Cartesian dualism. Metaphors are enacted in the thinking part of the body – the brain; the rest of the body is considered a physical encumbrance that can be abused or adored, neglected or pampered. Autoethnographers attempt to reunite the Cartesian split by embodying the experiences rather than just psychologising them. That is how Sparkes (1996, p. 477) comes to juxtapose his 'aching back' with the 'nagging feelings of insecurity' in 'The Fatal Flaw', in which he creates links between his working-class insecurities and his body.

Metaphors serve three purposes: first, as distillation they condense information that would require longer exposition; second, evocation: they stimulate imaginative and emotive responses; and third, by conceptual construction they alter a subject's sensitivity that could not be conveyed by literal translation. Many people use jokes in this way to say something that they find difficult to portray seriously (Denham, 2000).

THE GARDEN

Thomas Berry sums up my own passionately held views that 'gardening is an active participation in the deepest mysteries of the universe ... the universe is a communion of subjects not a collection of objects'. The garden gives me the perfect metaphor to live by, epitomised in Glyck's (1997) *Twelve Lessons on Life I Learned from my Garden*; everything from '*appreciating the growth of winter*', which teaches me that when nothing appears to be happening on the surface, a great deal is going on underneath. I believe writing is like this, as my best ideas come when I wake up after a night's sleep. The idea that '*less is more*' was incorporated into a curriculum that I designed and co-wrote, wanting students to have less time cramming in information and more time reflecting on what they were doing and learning. Finally, '*learning to appreciate silence*' – if your mind is constantly filled with extraneous thoughts and mindless activities, there will be no place for new ideas and creative thoughts to enter. When writer's block seems to paralyse you or no ideas emerge, spend some time in silence and be aware of the seedlings of ideas that will emerge unbidden.

It is no surprise then that, in a further iteration of my story, I used a gardening metaphor, which likened the abuse at the heart of my story to a black virus. My life has been interwoven with experience of the health service as a job from where my knowledge of viruses emerges against the backdrop of gardening as a hobby.

WINDOWSILL OF LIFE

I feel like a plant on the windowsill of life. Perched on this ledge I look forlornly in two directions. The darkness of the room forces me to reach to the light beyond the window and yet through the window the distance of the horizon compels me to seek the comfort of the claustrophobic room. I have never truly felt part of either world. In the dark and dingy room I struggle to find light and nourishment. Sustenance comes from the relics of a lifetime that surround me; the photos, the childish mementoes, the table, around which chatter and laughter accompanied celebrations with food. In this room silence now hangs like a brittle shroud, all-encompassing and yet elusive to touch; sometimes like a menacing black cloud, and at other times an all-consuming silence that envelopes me in its suffocating hold.

Despite never quite receiving the correct balance of nutrients, I put down long roots. These roots reached out into the orchards of my childhood, gently entwined round each other. Just as the mistletoe depends on the tree for survival and yet deprives it of vital nourishing ingredients, I clung on to a family who appeared to care on the surface but who squeezed out the essence of my childhood. These roots gave me the strength and motivation to survive but provided no extra strength to blossom and shine. In these early days I showed great promise. My foliage was lush and green, vigorous leaves would be produced, strong and full of potential, but the promise of full bloom seemed not to be in my grasp.

It was during these early years that a black virus pervaded the centre of my being. It came silently into my life, a shadowy figure, hardly tangible, but as persistent as any malignant cell. It cleverly recoded my blueprint for survival, leaving my outward appearance with a semblance of normality that would defy the damage that lay just below the surface. The tangle of my roots curled round the damage, trapping it in a web of deceit. I was programmed to believe that to blossom was just beyond my grasp and that struggle for survival was the only way to be. That black virus was not strong enough to overcome my motivation to survive, but it was as if it had entered my genetic code and become the blueprint for my personality – a thriving plant that as a result of this dark pervasive virus would be destined never to blossom.

~

TECHNIQUE TO STIMULATE IMAGINATION

Jones (2006, p. 66) points to the distrust of imagination and the 'knowledge diffusion' that has been severely limited to the written text or the omnipresent PowerPoint and needs development to conceptualise reports and presentations in 'dynamic vehicles' in order to liberate and transform the experience of individuals from exclusion to participation. Enlightenment comes from the sum of experience that has preceded the experience under scrutiny and the process of writing itself. It is within this complex framework of juxtapositions and memories that I share some suggestions for justification for, and development of, creatively transforming experience.

PICTURE 2   TESSA AGED 2 YEARS

Inspiration to write can come from the memorabilia that surround the experience you want to write about. The following exercise has been created without revision and is intended to show how thoughts can develop. Drafting, editing and rewriting are also part of the creative process.

Literal Description

It is not possible to leap from a school report or photograph to a full-blown metaphor or perfect poem. The first thing to do is to take some time to describe your artefacts and/or photos in detail. Take Picture 2, it is a rectangular photo, 6x4 cm, little girl, holding hands, dressed in a nurse's outfit, knee raised. Two years old, red cross, frilly armbands, face in profile, sunshine, coquettish pose. (*Added later*) orchard, summer day.

Imaginative Participation

Then, sit comfortably looking at your picture or object for a few moments and note down the first thing that comes into your mind, then repeat this as may times as you can by focusing on different aspects, using all of your senses: feelings, thoughts, memories, tastes, smells, sounds. Jot down the key words or brief description.

Dressed up for the coronation, orchard of my childhood, subliminal desire to be a nurse, rosy cheeks, brotherly love, adoration, gendered image (*added later*) smell of apple blossom, clucking of chickens, flash of cats' eyes, the silent glide of the 'old lady'.

Descriptive Prose

Think about the links between these statements or observations, and write a paragraph about this.

On a warm June afternoon I am attired in fancy dress to celebrate the coronation of our present queen. With no thought yet of nursing as a career, I am content to succumb to the fantasies of my mother, who must have chosen these clothes for me. As I hold hands with my brother – dressed as Andy Pandy – there is no hint of the menace that will eventually overwhelm me. With my knee cocked in joyful anticipation of the party in the village, there is no hint yet of the frightening meeting with the clown.

2nd attempt after some added thoughts and a period of reflection.

On a warm June afternoon, with the smell of late apple blossom in the orchard, I am attired in fancy dress in preparation for attendance at a party to celebrate the coronation of our present queen. Cats' eyes flash and chickens cluck contentedly in the long grass. With no thought yet of nursing as a career, I am content to succumb to the fantasies of my mother, who must have chosen these clothes for me. As I hold hands with my brother, who is dressed as Andy Pandy, there is no hint of the menace that will eventually overwhelm me. With my knee cocked in joyful anticipation of the party in the village, there is no hint yet of the frightening meeting with the clown. In the background the old lady glides silently amongst the trees, menacingly attired all in black, embodying a foreboding of my vulnerability.

Cut Up Technique

A further creative strategy is described by Biley (2004, pp. 139–49) wherein he adapts the cut up technique for disturbing the 'partial nature of any representation of reality that attempts to explore, describe or explain reality' (Cheek, 2000, p. 5).

 1 On a warm June afternoon,
 2 with the smell of late apple blossom in the orchard,
 3 I am attired in fancy dress
 4 in preparation for attendance at a party
 5 to celebrate the coronation of our present queen.
 6 Cats' eyes flash and chickens cluck
 7 contentedly in the long grass.
 8 With no thought yet of nursing as a career,
 9 I am content to succumb to the fantasies
 10 of my mother who must have chosen these clothes for me.
 11 As I hold hands with my brother
 12 who is dressed as Andy Pandy
 13 there is no hint of the menace
 14 that will eventually overwhelm me.
 15 With my knee cocked in joyful anticipation of the party in the village
 16 there is no hint yet of the frightening meeting with the clown.
 17 In the background the old lady glides silently amongst the trees
 18 menacingly attired all in black
 19 embodying a foreboding of my vulnerability.

Using a simple random sort in Excel (for a free trial download from http://www.digdb.com/excel_add_ins/random_sort_select/)

> 1 On a warm June afternoon
>
> 3 I am attired in fancy dress
>
> 8 with no thought yet of nursing as a career
>
> 17 In the background the old lady glides silently amongst the trees
>
> 4 in preparation for attendance at a party
>
> 2 with the smell of late apple blossom in the orchard
>
> 12 who is dressed as Andy Pandy
>
> 13 there is no hint of the menace
>
> 14 that will eventually overwhelm me
>
> 16 there is no hint yet of the frightening meeting with the clown
>
> 7 contentedly in the long grass
>
> 6 Cat's eyes flash and chickens cluck
>
> 19 embodying a foreboding of my vulnerability
>
> 5 to celebrate the coronation of our present queen
>
> 11 As I hold hands with my brother
>
> 9 I am content to succumb to the fantasies
>
> 18 menacingly attired all in black
>
> 10 of my mother who must have chosen these clothes for me
>
> 15 With my knee cocked in joyful anticipation of the party in the village

Write each sentence on a new line with a space in between. Then cut up to make a poem (Biley, 2004). *Then rewrite it tidying it up for ease of reading.*

With a bit of poetic licence, I transform my piece of writing into this, which I am prompted to call 'Suffocating June'.

On a warm June afternoon
I am attired in fancy dress
With no thought yet of nursing as a career.
In the background the old lady glides silently amongst the trees
in preparation for attendance at a party.

With the smell of late apple blossom in the orchard,
who is dressed as Andy Pandy?
There is no hint of the menace
that will eventually overwhelm me.
There is no hint yet of the frightening meeting with the clown.

Contentedly in the long grass.
Cats' eyes flash and chickens cluck
embodying a foreboding of my vulnerability.
To celebrate the coronation of our present queen
I hold hands with my brother

I am content to succumb to the fantasies
Menacingly attired all in black is my mother
who must have chosen these clothes for me.

But for now my is knee cocked in joyful anticipation
of the party in the village

~

I am particularly intrigued by the transformation of the old lady in black into my mother and the hint of darkness that this represents. I think it juxtaposes the innocence and vulnerability of my childhood with hints of the menace to come.

What follows is a reconstruction of my Windowsill of life text, which led me to rethink it as 'Blueprint for Survival'.

WINDOWSILL OF LIFE REVISITED

'Blueprint for Survival'

It came silently into my life,
trapped in a web of deceit.
A shadowy figure
It cleverly recoded my blueprint for survival
and became the blueprint for my personality.
It was not strong enough, this dark pervasive virus.
It left my outward appearance with a tangle of roots curled round the damage.
But it was as if it had entered my genetic code
and I would be destined to never blossom.
I was programmed to believe that I would never
defy the damage
and that struggle for survival was the only way to be.
A thriving plant during the early years.
Before a black virus
with a semblance of normality
and as pervasive as any malignant cell
meant that to blossom was just beyond my grasp
Just below the surface
hardly tangible
overcoming my motivation to survive
pervading the centre of my being.

SONGS

Transforming data into song lyrics is another fascinating way to present people's stories in a meaningful way. In Chapter 7, I show how David Carless explores the writing of songs and demonstrates parallels between transforming experience into song with experience into an autoethnography. Below is a song that resulted from the collection of data in a research project that he and Kitrina Douglas carried out for the Women's Sports Foundation in 2004 called 'Across the Tamar – Stories from

Women in Cornwall' (Douglas and Carless, 2005a; Douglas and Carless, 2005b). This song can be heard on David's web-space at http://www.myspace.com/davidcarless. The rhythm of the tune resonates with the rhythm of the woman climbing the stairs one step at a time.

'One Step at a Time'[1]

> There's some days when I come in
> and walk through my front door
> I rest there in the stairwell
> good foot, bad foot on the floor
> And I know, after all this time
> I cannot go on
>
> My mother when she struggled
> offered prayer up to the Lord
> So I follow my mother
> inside my front door
>
> That's what I do, my mother's child
> I pray to God
> Chorus:
> Then I climb the stairs
> Yes, I climb the stairs
> I climb the stairs
> One step at a time
>
> Grandchildren on the mantle
> and sons up on the wall
> Three brothers, three sisters
> just us two left that's all
> My husband gone, so long
> How to carry on?
>
> I'm going to climb the stairs
> Yes, I'll climb the stairs
> I'll climb the stairs
> One step at a time

STARTING TO WRITE

Now it is your turn. You've opened up a new document on the PC, your hands are poised over the keyboard – or you have opened up a new page in your journal and selected your favourite pen to write with – and what happens? A myriad of feelings: anticipation, excitement, anxiety, panic, unworthiness, and worst of all, nothing.

---

1 *Lyrics and music © David Carless, 2005*

Writing is often considered to be one of the hardest activities in the research process. If creativity is added to this experience, then the blank page can seem even more daunting. Although Virginia Woolf reminds us that 'Meaning lies on the far side of language .., (and) it is meaning which in moments of astonishing excitement and stress we perceive in our minds without words' (Woolf, 1966, p. 7). It is only with words or pictures or music that we can convey our ideas to others, to allow them to share our sense of our meaning.

Writing is not just a physical phenomenon. I want to introduce you to what Bachelard might call a phenomenology of writing, the actual experience of writing. Bachelard (1994, p. xxvi) suggests that in our passion for reading we 'nurture ... the desire to become a writer' however 'when the page we have just read is too near perfection, our modesty suppresses this desire'. How many of us consider the final polished versions of texts and forget the hours of drafting and redrafting, blood sweat and tears that they all entail. In being honest about the process, I want to reassure you that the stuttering starts, the periods of indecision, and the lapses of confidence with occasional surges of activity are the norm and should reassure you in beginning your own writing journey.

REFLECTIONS ON STARTING TO WRITE

Starting to write is a story in its own right. The enthusiastic attention to the kitchen floor is never usually felt in anything other than the manic few hours before guests are expected for the weekend. The dissatisfaction and annoyance of the vigorous weeds that are defying all gardening laws to grow successfully in the cracks of the patio draw me to them armed with a sharp knife to curtail their brief lives. Daffodils weep in folds of distress following the sharp frost of the night, but the intransigent weed grows stronger and sturdier. Whilst swishing the mop over lino and tiles and gouging the mercenary weeds from the patio crevices, I dodge backwards and forwards to a torn envelope on the kitchen table. With a blunt pencil I capture the scenes that emerge, full of sensory experiences and context, but with no clear characters. The only dialogue appears in my head. I feel no need to consider transition mechanisms between scenes; as yet this appears a luxury. If only characters would emerge full of teasing, intriguing dialogue, the vast scenery of my imagination could start to be used. I have exciting images from around the world against which the dilemmas could unfold; the metaphors from my garden could fill the crevices of my story, just as those weeds do, with ease.

The daunting task is opening up a new document and finding an opening sentence. But, just before I do that why don't I re-read extracts from other bits of writing. I've written before, surely I can do it again. I'd forgotten 'The handbag', that microcosm of my daily life and the 'windowsill of life', the yearning to be a big blousy peony instead of the vigorous green leaves that never blossomed. There's the journey along the River Nene watching England at war and at peace: the war being the fierce competition between the fishermen as they battled over who should have which pitch for their fishing match; and the peace being the silent floating parachutes over the Fens that gave the impression of an invasion into the soft, receptive landscape of the marshy land. Ironic that fishing is associated with tranquillity, and parachutes the precursor to capturing enemy territory in wartime. Did I really take three items, yellow washing-up gloves, red rose perfume and swimming cap, and weave them into an evocative tale of lost love in the First World War? Rose-tinted memories induced Proustian-like memories for Ethel and her lost love, Maurice.

My imagination gave birth to Ethel and Maurice so I'm not incapable of creating names for characters, so perhaps it's OK to start with descriptions of items and let characters emerge. Perhaps the characters are the many sides of me; perhaps I don't even have to be human. Could I be a plant in a children's story; could I be the swans that I watched for two days as they carefully protected the eggs from which the cygnets eventually emerged? If I were a plant I'd be a foxglove, abundant and undeterred by environmental constraints: slow to mature but a constant surprise as to the exact hue of my bonnet shaped leaves; content to grow anywhere but keen to snuggle up to the protective shelter of other plants. What gardener would plan to sow seeds in the concrete cracks of a path? But there the foxglove will flourish. Alternatively, the evening primrose that flowers abundantly on the scree of the drive seems to say 'look, I don't need much to survive but I do want to be alone, unencumbered by other plants'. Are these clues to my characters or just continued distractions from the blank page of a new story?

After yet another deviation to read selections of my mother's writing about kitchens and motherhood, I'm starting to see a structure of rooms in a house that could be the shape of my story. Events taking part in the various rooms plus the garden could evolve into a tale of false trails and accusations of false memories. Why don't I start with the kitchen and see where it takes me? Can't see much of a genre emerging, haven't really considered myself a crime writer, so don't really want a murder in the bathroom. A ghost might be a corny twist but I'm intrigued by the idea of a ghost lurking in the corridors that connect the rooms in some way. Couldn't a ghost also be part of the alter ego of the present occupier? House as a prison? The world as a view from the window? Themes of second chances or healthy environments? What about working towards a last line: 'Closing the front door with a desultory glance over her shoulder, Phoebe shook off the ghosts that had inveigled their way into her life and set off for a new life on board her narrowboat "Raven"'. It seems an anomaly that the tiny space of her new life should be so much less claustrophobic than the rooms that had seemed so expansive to her as a child.

If I can write 850 words of reflection, surely I can write the same amount of words as a beginning – perhaps I'll just have lunch before I do!

~

This is a piece of creative writing undertaken while on a creative writing course. It was not intended for publication and I didn't anticipate that the merits or otherwise of its content and style might be judged. I wanted to try and display the frustration, ambivalence, reflexivity, and sheer excuses that enter into the writing process. I was also responding to Cameron's (1995) advice that when you are stuck, just start writing whatever comes into your mind. However, having selected it to put into a text that is to be published, it has moved beyond being just a personal experience. It now has an audience, who will judge it and question its position and authority, or just suspect the sheer point of it. This raises important points about the intended audience for a piece of writing and just as importantly its timing. Sparkes's (2007) damning indictment of the Research Assessment Exercise (RAE) portrayed in his fictional account of the mental and physical breakdown of Jim from the University of Wannabee Academic as a result of the RAE, not only had to be published in a peer reviewed journal to be worthy of inclusion in his RAE submission but had to be published in time to meet the deadline. In an interview for the Times Higher Education Supplement he says 'it is a fictional narrative but it rings true with people' (Corbyn, 2007). Ringing true or resonating is an important quality of this kind of writing. Sparkes's paper also represents an anti-establishment view with the distinctive pleasure of contributing to the very process it is attempting to criticise. This demonstrates that the style, the reason for writing, the timing and its potential impact all contribute to the development of a piece; but one thing that cannot be escaped is that this genre of writing is intended for publication and, in the purpose and process of publication, writing becomes changed in the process.

I'm reminded of the philosophical conundrum as to whether we know that the light stays on when we close the fridge door. Understanding the mechanics of the on/off switch mechanism may convince some; others may require proof by considering ways of being in the fridge when the door shuts; and others may just say who cares as long as the light comes on when I open the door, so that I can select my food. Still others may just enjoy the philosophical debate in its own right. Readers of academic papers fall into these categories. There is an assumption that a paper will provide proof of a concept, conclusions and evidence, and rarely will the reader be left to make up their own mind. The pragmatist may just be looking for evidence to support their own ideas, and the debate is neatly tied up with precise conclusions within the confines of the paper. Autoethnography challenges these assumptions while still having to meet the challenges of the publishing world, including the review process, which I will return to in the next chapter.

WRITING PHASES

This piece of writing was a stream of consciousness activity to try to get myself beyond the paralysis of getting started on a new piece of writing. It is interesting that as I start to write a commentary about this process, I start to feel the same anxieties and lack of confidence that gave rise to the need to do it in the first place. Getting started is perhaps the most arduous part of the process; when in full flow the only problem becomes the need to eat and sleep and be sociable with one's family. I have divided the writing process up into five distinct phases, each with their own discrete characteristics, namely: Cognitive, Scribbling, Serious, Polishing and Relishing. Recognising these phases should help to reassure you as you stumble backwards and forwards through the process to the finished product. As with all processes, they may not happen in a linear fashion, they may all happen in one day or you may get stuck at any one stage. A consideration of each stage will identify the associated characteristics and perhaps some remedies if stuck for longer than comfortable. Being comfortable is a key characteristic of each stage because when no activity is happening this can be construed as a failure. However, you should be reminded that, just as the silence of winter is a necessary prerequisite for the growth of plants in the spring, so inactivity in the writing process can be a prerequisite for stimulating the imagination – a time to reflect, read the work of others or just rest.

Cognitive Phase

At this stage you are full of confidence and enthusiasm for an idea you have to write. You have just completed an academic study or have the promise of a trip to an exciting conference, if you can only get a paper underway. You may have completed an inspiring teaching session or lecture that you have been encouraged to publish to a wider audience. You may be enraged by the sentiments of a paper or a newspaper article or the results of a piece of research, and you compose articulate arguments to counteract the injustice you see. This may also be the starting point for your autoethnography, but more of that in the next chapter. You take to allowing long streams of consciousness to preoccupy you, especially when your mind is freed by activities that don't require any cognitive involvement; anything from washing-up, to walking the dog, to gardening, and swimming.

During this phase no one else knows of your plans to write, you probably have no deadline looming and if you never get beyond this stage no one will know and you will have lost no self respect or esteem. While everything remains a figment of your imagination, you do not have to dread the ignominy of the critical reviewer or the slight of rejection by the commissioning editor, or having your abstract rejected by the scientific committee of the conference. This phase ends when your ideas emerge into the ether. You make a few notes, you maybe confide in a colleague or a friend and the idea becomes a tangible thing.

Scribbling Phase

This is a messy phase. The ideas have stopped flowing quite so fluently or they are so abundant that you can't keep up with them. Either way, you know you have to start to write things down. You may be one of life's very organised minority who never leave home without a notebook and a well-documented diary, but usually these ideas will come when you are otherwise engaged. More of my scribbles are recorded on backs of envelopes as I wander in from the garden and reach the first scrap of paper I can find, although for the purposes of this writing exercise I am keeping a diary (see below). Selection of a diary provided an interesting digression, as I found a notebook used by my youngest son and a short reverie of his use of the textbook swallowed up some more valuable time.

You should be aware here that translating thoughts into text changes them. In your imagination they flow seamlessly, just like the response you rehearse to an argument the day after it has occurred. However, writing them down is a necessary start to the process, as it releases your imagination to move on to other thoughts. Unrecorded, they wear out a groove in your thinking that not only stifles your creativity but begins to bore you. Ideas may be stimulated by a novel you are reading, a newspaper article, or a quote; you may suddenly remember a reference you want to look up, or remind yourself to contact someone by email or phone. Some of my best thoughts come either first thing in the morning, after a period of sleep, or occupy my waking thoughts in the middle of the night. I have learned that the best way to get back to sleep is to write them down. Your partner may take a dim view of your putting on the light, so this may mean getting up for a short while, but it is an important task, not to be avoided. Scribbling is intended to control anxiety, which grows inexorably the nearer you get to committing yourself to the project. These scribbles may sit undisturbed for a long time. You may want to start a folder labelled 'writing ideas' to store them for future use, and you'll certainly rediscover the scraps of paper and tattered envelopes when you start to tidy up, which brings me neatly to the next phase, where tidying up becomes the most important thing you must do.

Serious Phase

As I've intimated, this is often the point of no return, where any other activity known to you suddenly becomes more important than settling down to write – washing the kitchen floor, paying bills, writing to old friends, turning out the attic, watching that TV programme you recorded; and the ultimate indicator of imminent writing activity for me – cleaning up my writing space. For weeks and months I am surrounded by clutter, papers to review, marking to comment on, lists to do and things I just don't know whether to keep or throw away. Suddenly, it is vital that the papers are in alphabetical order and my filing system is updated to include the miscellaneous clutter.

You turn on the PC and open up a new document and … sometimes nothing happens. You know that opening sentences are vital, they set the mood, invite the reader in, and give a teasing indication of what is to come. You go back to your scribblings and try to formulate a plan. You spend an inordinate amount of time searching for an elusive reference on the internet and then grudgingly you return to the open document. To avoid this stultifying impasse, I usually wait till my opening sentence has formed in a cognitive phase. However, there is no substitute for just starting to write. Fluency comes when you let go of the censor in your thoughts. You will not be judged on this first draft; after all that thinking and scribbling there are lots of ideas waiting to be expressed.

Polishing Phase

Once you have completed a draft and sent it off to sympathetic colleagues for comment, you will probably have had enough. The enthusiasm dwindles and you just want it published. Each rereading shows there are many other ways you could have done it. You may be very proud of some bits and ashamed of others. Very often, the word count is exceeded and there follows the painful experience of removing some of those carefully crafted words. This is like pulling out your own teeth. Perhaps an elusive quote does not materialise and you have no option but to remove it. I am reminded at this stage of one such elusive quote by George Eliot, which I found cited by someone else and was determined to find the primary source. I tracked down the 1926 version of the book it was supposed to be in, and after reading the whole book, I found to my horror that it wasn't there. I was furious and vowed to lecture my students on the importance of accurate referencing. Undeterred, I set about reading anything I could find written about her, and one day in an airport bookshop I found a new book with the reference correctly cited. My sense of satisfaction was immense and my life the richer for reading about this fascinating author.

The polishing stage is full of frustrating diversions like this, but the real work is reserved for the review process. The academic world favours the blind review. This sometimes allows complete strangers to say what they like about your work with no redress by yourself. They can be both cruel and constructive but they remain between you and the public domain. Editors do their best to match up reviewers to papers but in the world of autoethnography the circle is limited. Finding critical friends for yourself, someone you trust to give honest feedback, can be useful; also, try to offer your own services as a critical friend, as this can be a good way of learning.

Relishing Phase

This is an unpredictable phase that I added after one my reviewers, Jeni Boyd, described herself as feeling astounded at what I had written; could I really have said/thought done that? However, this may be followed very swiftly by 'doubt' and 'diffidence'. With the passage of time, your work may seem naïve, or overtaken by more developed thought; and I have always thought it a very healthy feeling to leave a piece of work knowing that it could have been done a different way or could be developed further. However, for a short while you should at least allow yourself to blossom in the context of a job well done.

AIDS TO SUCCESSFUL WRITING

Jane Austen did all her writing on a tiny table positioned by a squeaking door so she could stop if someone came into the room. While hopefully you will not be as constrained as Austen, it is important to have a dedicated space in which to write. Halfway through my PhD I moved house and was almost paralysed by fear that I wouldn't be able to work in a new environment.

Diaries

Good ideas come at inopportune moments, often while you're distracted by mundane tasks. So I think the keeping of a diary is vital. The uses of a diary are potentially vast.

They can be straightforward chronicling of events, or bald record of facts. They can be confessional, or cathartic, or an opportunity to vent one's spleen. However, in terms of creative writing, they can become a canvas on which to record experimental ideas, an attempt to impose some sort of order on the chaos. While the discipline of recording may at first be arduous, you will eventually find you have an identity of your own and that it will glow with the immediacy of your everyday thoughts.

My book diary contains quotes, references to books, spontaneous ideas, words that have appeared in conversation with others, and these come unbidden and need to be captured so that they are not forgotten. In *The Artist's Way*, Julia Cameron (1995) recommends writing at least three morning pages every day. These are pages of free style script, like a writing diary, that just get you into the habit of committing your ideas to paper. Writing is a skill that needs to be practised to become more effective. I can remember when I first started to write my morning pages, deliberating as to how big the pages should be; should I write with a pen or a pencil; could the morning pages in fact be produced on the computer?

My First Diary Entry in July 1999

~

I've been deliberating all morning over starting this writing, doing all sorts of inconsequential things because it was putting off the moment of starting. While I was washing up, I was thinking, does this writing have to be longhand or can it be on the PC; will I still be able to write in longhand? Then I thought 'how long is three pages?' Does it mean three pages of a spiral notepad, quite small, like those in a shorthand notebook, or does it mean an exercise book? If the size of writing is small, then surely I will write a lot more than someone with big writing. All of this is suggesting that I need to know the rules and boundaries of the exercise, that I constantly need to compare what I do myself with what others are doing.

~

Of course, captured in this tiny fragment is a revelation of my insecurity and need for boundaries that underpins every thing that I do. These are of course the deliberations of the internal evaluator, ever ready to criticise, who has to be by-passed in order to create. I suggest that it doesn't matter at the start what you write with, and in trying different writing implements you might find you create something quite different. Actively writing ideas that have been on your mind before sleep need to be captured first thing in the morning, so keep a pad ready by the bed. Despite the luxury of a personal computer and the ease of writing something that can so easily be edited, I have never quite lost the fascination for writing in pencil, which for me brings a closer relationship between the words and the sentiment. Finally, with the invention of electronic referencing software, there is no excuse for losing references. EndNote 'Cite While You Write' facility has transformed the chore of citation and referencing in my work, and I cannot recommend it or other similar programs strongly enough.

WHO ARE WE WRITING FOR?

The review process is intended to maintain standards in academic publishing. Editors select two or three people with expertise in a related field, who provide comment on the paper using a range of criteria. They recommend publication with a variety of options, including resubmission with suggested changes to the text. I am intrigued by this process with an autoethnographic text, because the text is deemed to be the individual's personal experience and should set out its own criteria for judgement. Is it intended to create controversy, as in Sparkes's piece about the RAE; or to provoke an alternative explanation, as in Wall's (2008) attempt to subvert the dominant discourse of international adoption; or to evoke an empathy for those whose voices are not heard in the hidden experience of suicide, as in Isaac (2007)? Whatever the intention, it is the reviewer who will have first say, and they and the editor exert a powerful hold over whether or not your piece is published. Credibility becomes entangled with legitimacy and the review process becomes part of the story.

Reporting research has a very standardised format and autoethnography challenges these traditional writing conventions. Gingrich-Philbrook (2005, p. 297) refers to this as the 'double bind between the epistemic and aesthetic demands of autoethnography and autoethnographic performance'. In this double bind, the writer requires 'a willingness to confront the place of personal writing as a producer and carrier of "knowledge" at a time when what constitutes knowledge is somewhat in doubt' (Gingrich-Philbrook, 2005, p. 298).

The reporting conventions of published work can make the reviewer feel safe and, by contrast, the unconventional can be challenging and uncomfortable. Some authors have incorporated the review process into their writing or even made it the focus of the piece, often referred to as writing stories (Richardson, 1995). This is demonstrated to very good effect in Holt's (2003) critique of representation and legitimation relating to the review process of his own autoethnographic writing. He writes of the process of rejection and resubmission of his piece of work and the suspicious, sceptical, albeit sympathetic, responses that he received.

As I write this I am struck by the conventions that this text also is adhering to, so that the reader will not feel alienated from the process. I am referring to authors by their last names even though I know some of them better by their first names. Imagine the chaos of only using first names when a whole industry has been devoted to the use of the surname. My reference manager software certainly wouldn't cope. I remember at a conference Harry Wolcott (2001) questioning the conventions of writing theses and dissertations; wherever you go in the world, he said, the second chapter will always be the literature review, the justification that what is being considered has a theoretical, methodological, ontological and epistemological justification, even though the study probably emanated from a professional hunch or an event in the author's experience.

Grounded theory is perhaps the only approach where a justification is made for not first looking at the literature, although we cannot disassociate ourselves from the professional reading that we have already done as part of our work. However, Heath (2006) suggests that in any study all selections are arbitrary and incomplete. This need to situate our qualitative research writing within the conventions of a methodology seems to have stemmed from concerns about the quality of the work.

I realise that to write with any authority, commitment and enthusiasm one has to believe in the ideas beyond the cognitive knowing level to an intuitive belief level. When I am not fully committed, I find that I have a tendency to hide behind the voices of others, and from time to time I situate my own ideas within those voices, recognising that often it is the voices of others that have influenced the views that I hold. However, I don't believe I ever lose sight of the fact that stories are a 'form of social action' (Atkinson and Delamont, 2006).

How could I forget that my experience of teenage pregnancy has to be viewed through a sociopolitical lens that finds no positive attributes in the experience and places the blame squarely on my own shoulders? How can I distance myself from a history that at one time would have seen me incarcerated in a mental institution or be relieved that I live in a culture that doesn't punish. But I don't quite understand what they are worried about when they suggest that 'we cannot proceed as if they (narratives) were privileged accounts, or as if they gave the writer and the reader access to the private domain of personal experience' (Atkinson and Delamont, 2006, p. 170). I would agree that the powerless and the powerful deserve 'close analytic attention' but am very mindful that the powerful voice is privileged and that while there is no level playing field for those differing views, the powerless need to find more imaginative ways to capture attention.

After some consideration of their views, I think that Atkinson and Delamont among many others are merely providing a very sophisticated retort to the claim of autoethnography being just a form of self indulgence. Mykhalovskiy (1996, p. 131) uses irony to expose how self indulgence 'considers highly insular relations of readership, authorship and subject/object distinction' which rely heavily on the traditional masculine academic discourse.

After all, storytelling is one of the oldest worldwide traditions with an infinite variety of wisdoms and techniques; storytelling is synonymous with song, chant, music, or epic poetry, and artists have always fulfilled the roles of spiritual teachers, historians and tradition-bearers. Science, with its desire for objectivity, tended to silence the storyteller. Perhaps the autoethnographer is just trying to put stories back, albeit in forms that recognise the conventions of the age in which they are told.

OTHER WRITERS ON WRITING

In the foreword to *The Writer's Handbook*, Barry Turner (2004) makes a plea for clarity in writing and speaking; he cites Fritz Spiegel (Turner, 2004, p. 3) who says 'Words are precious tools. You can use a screwdriver as a chisel but it will never be the same again'. Turner is particularly critical of the way the social sciences obfuscate (or in plain English make something difficult to understand). Good writing is like good teaching: words should be clear to the intended audience. This does not mean reducing all jargon to simple words but only using concepts that have a shared understanding between the writer and the intended audience.

Writers grapple with many distractions and concerns in the process of writing. The need for support in this process is evident in the list of acknowledgements which, once *de rigueur* in heavily researched, non-fiction writing, now also appears in novels. This is an indication that, although the novel uses words to portray an illusion of reality, the fictitious account must be recognisable to the reader. In some cases, novels draw on the author's own experience to the point where fiction and non-fiction blurs. For example it is known that *Great Expectations* was based partly on Dickens's own life, and that Daniel Defoe's *Robinson Crusoe* was suggested by and even based on real events. The popularity of Khaled Hosseini's book *A Thousand Splendid Suns* is due not only to the exquisite writing but also to the idea that the reader believes they are seeing something of the historic events in Afghanistan and their impact on the lives of women in the last thirty years. The demise of Mariam is probably one of the most evocative pieces of writing I have encountered for a while, a very good example where showing is far more powerful than telling.

Mariam's final thoughts were a few words from the Koran, which she muttered under her breath.

'He has created the heavens and the earth with the truth; He makes the night cover the day and makes the day overtake the night, and He has made the sun and the moon subservient; each one runs on to an assigned term; now surely He is the Mighty, the Great Forgiver.'

'Kneel,' the Talib said.

'O my Lord! Forgive and have mercy, for you are the best of the merciful ones.'

'Kneel here, *hamshira*. And look down.'

One last time, Mariam did as she was told. (Hosseini, 2008, p. 361)

Choices always have to be made about what to include or leave out of any piece of writing. For example despite being hailed as one of the original and most popular of the realist novels, Jane Austen's (1998 [1813]) *Pride and Prejudice* has been criticised by some because of its complete denial of the Peninsular War, which was happening at the time that she was writing.

This dilemma of choosing what to include or leave out in writing is compounded by the sheer volume and contradictory nature of the information available. In her introduction to *The Duchess,* a biography of Georgiana, Duchess of Devonshire, Foreman explores her dilemma in seeking the truth about her subject. Following an immersion in the artefacts of the subject such as letters, diaries and even discarded fragments 'the truth is maddeningly elusive. The subject's own self deception, mistaken recollections and the hidden motives of witnesses conspire to make a complete picture impossible to assemble' (Foreman, 2008, p. xiii). I would argue that this is not applicable just to biography, but that the autobiographer and autoethnographer writing about themselves are also subject to the same diversions and dilemmas. Foreman provides one answer to this conundrum when she admits that for her 'it is intuition and a sympathy with the past which supply the last missing pieces' (Foreman, 2008, p. xiii).

All writing has to be considered in context. My experience of teenage pregnancy happened at a time when abortion was still illegal, but after the time when young women were incarcerated in asylums for getting pregnant outside marriage. It has to be set alongside the upheavals in social reform in the 1960s, before the widespread availability of the contraceptive pill and the influence of the second wave of feminism. This sociocultural lens through which all writing must be viewed explains why early biographies of Virginia Woolf do not mention her sexual abuse (Lee, 1997).

The parallels between autoethnographic accounts and the descriptions used by authors writing novels are very clear. Authors interviewed at the Cheltenham Book Festival in 2007 hinted at the unconscious, almost irrational, aspect of creating stories, together with some of the practicalities that keep them focused (Wark, 2007). They describe it as a vocation, an impulse, a relationship tangled up with visual art, a contribution from the unconscious mind or a process of meditation.

VOICE

Carol Gilligan's seminal text *In a Different Voice* introduced me to the complex theories of which voices come to be heard, in psychological theory in particular (Gilligan, 1993). Voice is not just about speaking, speech patterns, volume and intonation, but is the whole panoply of language and ideas that is articulated in theories and texts purporting to represent everybody's experience. Gilligan was drawing attention to the lack of women's perspective in the canon of psychological literature; and Jean Baker Miller tried to fashion a psychology for women that aimed to 'create a way of life that includes serving others without being subservient' (Baker Miller, 1988, p. 72). Gilligan (1993, p. xv) suggests 'to have a voice is to be human, to have something to say is to be a person'. Speaking depends on listening and being heard; and the social sciences have tended to be deaf to some particular voices.

The presentation of a voice in a piece of text may well link to the difference between saying and telling. There is nothing wrong with telling your reader something, but it can keep them in a passive position with nothing to bring them into the action or left to imagine or construct for themselves. It is usually better to show them through hints and descriptions, then they can become immersed in the moment.

Many of the voices we hear are of articulate, educated groups of people. One striking example of a different voice can be found in a novel by Jill Miller (1983) called *Happy as a Dead Cat*. The opening paragraph reads:

> If shitface asks me what I do with the housekeeping money once more, I'll carve him up with the pissing bread knife. (I happened to be washing up at the time. Had I been hanging out the clothes on the line I dare say I would have thought of strangling the bleeder.) (Miller, 1983, p. 1)

You don't have to be told what is happening in this women's marriage, of her anger and frustration; the tone and language speak volumes.

To present your experience in an imaginative engaging way requires you to experiment with and find your own voice.

Summary

- Writing requires strategies.
- Creativity requires serious commitment and practice.
- Artistic tools need to be used with respect to literary and poetic conventions.
- Snapshots are only a skeleton of a life, they are memory teasers.
- Artefacts convey significance and stimulate imagination.
- Poetry can trouble both the conscious and the unconscious into looking at new ways of reflecting on experience.
- Metaphors serve to distil, evocate and alter sensitivities.
- Writers are people who write.
- Writing requires practice and progresses through distinct phases but not necessarily chronologically.
- Writing is always done for a particular audience.
- Voice is not just about speech and is portrayed more effectively by showing not telling.

FURTHER READING

Cameron, J. (1995) *The Artist's Way.* Pan Macmillan, Basingstoke.

Julia Cameron describes a whole twelve-week course for unlocking your creativity.

Richardson, L. (1990) *Writing Strategies: Reaching diverse audiences.* Sage, London.

Laurel Richardson expands on the craft of writing for diverse audiences with a consideration of literary devices and narrative structures.

Woods, P. (2006) *Successful Writing for Qualitative Researchers.* Routledge, Abingdon.

Peter Woods provides a thorough grounding in all aspects relating to translating research into writing, including a chapter called 'Alternative forms of representation' (ch. 4, pp. 43–64), where he provides an introduction to a range of experimental writing.

REFERENCES

Ahern, C. (2008) *Thanks for the Memories*. Harper Collins, London.

Atkinson, P. and Delamont, S. (2006) Rescuing narrative from qualitative research. *Narrative Inquiry*, **16**(1), 164–72.

Austen, J. (1998 [1813]) *Pride and Prejudice*. Oxford University Press, Oxford.

Bachelard, G. (1994) *The Poetics of Space*. Beacon Press, Boston, MA.

Baker Miller, J. (1988) *Toward a New Psychology of Women*. Penguin, Harmondsworth.

Barthes, R. (1981) *Camera Lucida: Reflections on photography*. Farrar, Straus and Giroux, New York.

Biley, F. (2004) Postmodern Literary Poetics of Experience: A new form of aesthetic enquiry. In F. Rapport (Ed.) *New Qualitative Methodologies in Health and Social Care Research*. Routledge, London, pp. 139–49.

Bilton, T., Bonnett, K., Jones, P., Lawson, T., Skinner, D., Stanworth, M. and Webster, A. (1996) *Introductory Sociology*. Palgrave Macmillan, Basingstoke.

Bohm, D. (2004) *On Creativity*. Routledge, Oxford.

Cameron, J. (1995) *The Artist's Way*. Pan Macmillan, Basingstoke.

Cheek, J. (2000) *Postmodern and Poststructural Approaches to Nursing Research*. Sage, London.

Corbyn, Z. (2007) '"Bollocks": RAE paper assesses the RAE'. *The Times Higher Education Supplement*, 7 December, p. 1.

Denham, A. (2000) *Metaphor and Moral Experience*. Clarendon Press, Oxford.

Derrida, J. (1978) *Writing and Difference*. Routledge and Kegan Paul, London.

Douglas, K. and Carless, D. (2005a) Across the Tamar – Stories from women in Cornwall. Retrieved November 2008, from http://www.acrossthetamar.co.uk/

Douglas, K. and Carless, D. (2005b) Older Women's Physical Activity in Rural Areas. Retrieved November 2008, from http://www.wsf.org.uk/docs/physical_activity_in_older_women.doc

Foreman, A. (2008) *The Duchess*. Harper Perennial, London.

Gilligan, C. (1993) *In a Different Voice*. Harvard University Press, Cambridge, MA.

Gingrich-Philbrook, C. (2005) Autoethnography's family values: Easy access to compulsory experiences. *Text and Peformance Quarterly*, **25**(4), 297–314.

Glyck, V. (1997) *Twelve Lessons on Life I Learned from My Garden*. Daybreak Books, Emmaus, PA.

Heath, H. (2006) Exploring the influences and use of the literature during a grounded theory study. *Journal of Research in Nursing*, **11**(6), 519–28.

Holt, N.L. (2003) Representation, legitimation, and autoethnography: An autoethnographic writing story. *International Journal of Qualitative Methods*, **2**(1), 1.

Hosseini, K. (2008) *A Thousand Splendid Suns*. Bloomsbury, London.

Isaac, C.A. (2007) By their own hand – irreconcilable silence. *Qualitative Inquiry*, **13**(8), 1209–20.

Jones, K. (2006) A biographic researcher in pursuit of an aesthetic: The use of arts-based (re)presentations in 'performative' dissemination of life stories. *Qualitative Sociological Review*, **11**(1), 66–85.

Kaysen, S. (2000) *Girl, Interrupted*. Virago, London.

Kingston, K. (1996) *Creating Sacred Space*. Piatkus, London.

Kompf, M. (1999) '"There is more to me than my story … " Examinations of what narrative researchers leave behind', paper presented at the 9th biennial meeting of the International Study Association on Teachers and Teaching, St Patrick's College, Dublin, July.

Lakoff, G. and Johnson, M. (1980) *Metaphors We Live by*. University of Chicago Press, Chicago, IL.

Lee, H. (1997) *Virginia Woolf*. Vintage, London.

Maltby, M. (2003) Wordless Words: Poetry and the symmetry of being. In H. Canham and C. Satyamurti (Eds) *Acquainted with the Night*. Karnac, London.

Miller, J. (1983) *Happy As a Dead Cat*. The Women's Press, London.

Muncey, T. (2000) Nursing Metaphors. In D. Freshwater (Ed.) *Making a Difference*. Nursing Praxis International, Nottingham, ch. 2.

Muncey, T. (2004) Doing Autoethnography: A patchwork life. In *Qualitative Research in Health and Social Care*. Bournemouth University, Bournemouth.

Muncey, T. (2005). Doing autoethnography. *International Journal of Qualitative Methods*, **4**(3), Article 5. Retrieved January 2009, from http://www.ualberta.ca/~iiqm/backissues/4_1/html/muncey.htm

Myerhoff, B. (1986) Life Not Death in Venice. In V. Turner and E. Bruner (Eds) *The Anthropology of Experience*. University of Illinois Press, Chicago, IL.

Mykhalovskiy, E. (1996) Reconsidering table talk: Critical thoughts on the relationship between sociology, autobiography and self-indulgence. *Qualitative Sociology*, **19**(1), 131–51.

Nidditch, P. (Ed.) (1975) *John Locke: An essay concerning human understanding*. Clarendon Press, Oxford.

Richardson, L. (1995) Writing-stories: Co-authoring 'The Sea Monster', a writing story. *Qualitative Inquiry*, **1**, 189.

Richardson, L. (2001) Getting personal: Writing-stories. *International Journal of Qualitative Studies in Education*, **14**(1), 33–8.

Romanyshyn, R. (1982) *Psychological Life: From science to metaphor*. The Open University Press, Milton Keynes.

Russell, C. (1999) *Experimental Ethnography*. Duke University Press, Durham, NC.

Sparkes, A.C. (1996) The fatal flaw: A narrative of the fragile body-self. *Qualitative Inquiry*, **2**, 463–93.

Sparkes, A.C. (2007) Embodiment, academics and the audit culture: A story seeking consideration. *Qualitative Research*, **7**(4), 521–50.

Speedy, J. (2005) Using poetic documents: An exploration of poststructuralist ideas and poetic practices in narrative therapy. *British Journal of Guidance & Counselling*, **33**(4), 283–98.

Turner, B. (Ed.) (2004) *The Writer's Handbook*. Macmillan, Basingstoke.

Walker, A. (2000) *The Color Purple*. The Women's Press, London.

Wall, S. (2008) Easier said than done: Writing an autoethnography. *International Journal of Qualitative Methods*, **7**.

Wark, P. (2007) 'Behind the lines', *The Times*, 9 October, p. 4.

Wittgenstein, L. (1953) *Philosophical Investigations*. Basil Blackwell, Oxford.

Wolcott, H.F. (2001) Writing up Qualitative Research ... Better. In *Advances in Qualitative Methods*. West Edmonton Mall, Edmonton, AB.

Woolf, V. (1966) On Not Knowing Greek. In L. Woolf, *Collected Essays*. Hogarth Press, London.

5
MAKING SENSE OF AUTOETHNOGRAPHIC TEXTS: Legitimacy, Truth and Memory

CHAPTER PREVIEW

Remembering
What memory research leaves out
Ethics
Truth and story

Up until this point, I have been keen to promote the positive elements in respect of creating autoethnographies, but tensions do exist and challenges will be inevitable. You may have produced a story, or a paper that you are ready to launch into a public space. You've interwoven your experience into your thesis, you are happy with the strength and consistency of your metaphor; your poems resonate with your critical readers and yet at the back of your mind is the ever present voice that says isn't this just self-indulgent nonsense? So you've arrived at this chapter with many questions about legitimacy running through your mind. All right, it might be more ingenuous to admit your position and include yourself in your work, or you might even be wholeheartedly using yourself as the focus of your study, but what about the nagging doubts about how to justify your creation? How do you answer the challenge about your memory of these perhaps historical events? Your truth will be questioned, as will the particular notion of the self that are you adopting.

Unless people were prepared to share their experiences, we would have no history to recall, as Cran and Robertson evocatively point out

> Go into any place where history is stored and listen. Hold your breath. Hear how still it is. Librarians and archivists will keep visitors quiet, but this particular silence has nothing to do with them. It runs through buzzing computer rooms and waits in busy record offices, it is always there. It is the sound of nothingness. It is the huge invisible, silent roar of all the people who are too small to record. They disappear and leave the past inhabited only by murderers and prodigies and saints. (Cran and Robertson, 1996, p. 185)

So to be able to hear the 'silent roar' of the invisible inevitably requires some risk-taking. Challenges to accepted ideas of legitimacy in research need to be considered alongside a reflection on the role of truth and memory in recollections about ourselves.

SIX RESPONSES TO MY STORY

Ah, but You're Different

The lecture theatre is packed. A sea of expectant faces turn towards me as I am introduced. I smile at some familiar faces and silently rehearse my opening line. My anxiety increases proportionately to the size of the audience and I reassure myself with the calming words of a colleague – 'if you can teach seven you can teach seventy'. But this isn't your average lecture, this is one that I have invested a lot of personal energy in and I feel slightly exposed. I've been invited to speak to a group of midwives and school nurses who are attending a study day on Teenage Pregnancy and I have a slight reputation for being provocative. I'm in the slot before dinner and as I pause before I start to speak, I remind myself that I am speaking for the silenced and silent majority, who do not have this opportunity to address a professional group who could make a difference. My resolve strengthens, I aim to be polemical, I have a colleague to debrief me afterwards, and I hear my voice ring out.

I confess that I am interested in the topic because of my work as a health visitor; my current preoccupation with writing a chapter on the topic; and that I am a teenage mother myself, what follows is a critique of the literature surrounding the topic, interspersed with my own story, which talks of the positive element of the experience and clearly sets out my thesis that teenage pregnancy should be considered within the paradigm of abuse. I'm not afraid to leave time for questions. I stop speaking and take another look at the audience. There is a woman just to the right of my eye line with her hand raised bursting to ask a question. I nod and smile and her statement explodes into the atmosphere. 'I want to disagree with almost everything you have said!' There is a gasp from the audience and I almost feel the walls of the lecture theatre being sucked in. This is not a statement she appears to want me to respond to as she continues, 'Teenage mothers are an economic drain on society and should be stopped at all costs'.

The tirade continues, and as I listen to the tired rhetoric she is spouting, I feel saddened that this is a midwife who on a daily basis will come into contact with this vulnerable group of young women, and I despair at the treatment they will receive. When she pauses, I am ready with my counterclaims. My pulse is racing and my voice is slightly disembodied. I hear myself refer her again to the statistics on childhood sexual abuse, and suggest that although this is not the only reason, it is a reason that is rarely considered. In response to her accusation that all teenage mothers are an economic drain, I admit to her that I have always been financially independent. 'Ah', she says magnanimously 'but of course you are different' and just as my body is attempting to recover from this absurd statement she delivers her punchline – 'where is the reward for girls that keep themselves nice!'

The audience erupts around me. I realise there is no easy answer to this sanctimonious tone but I feel the need to have the last word. I'm sure I say with as much control as I can muster ' I'm sure there are thousands of little girls out there living in unsafe households being abused by family members in unspeakable silence who would love the opportunity to keep themselves nice'. I pause and shuffle my notes and the audience files out to lunch, but I am heartened by a steady stream of individuals who approach me to distance themselves from that view and, as always, there are a few who want to share their own stories with me.

But it May Not Be True

A young female anthropologist, who was typical of many presenters I have listened to, is delivering her paper in a concurrent session at a conference. I am sitting in the audience with my hackles rising as I hear the same old discourse about teenage mothers; my heart starts to race and I know I am going to speak out. 'I'm a teenage mother' I say, and pause. I know the impact of this statement is one of incredulity, for I am in my early 50s, grey-haired and clearly not a teenager. 'When would you remove the label?' I ask, having admitted that I became pregnant at 15 with my first child.

This promotes an interesting debate but is not the main point I want to make. I wanted to break through what I felt was a smugness about the obviousness in the shared view of researchers about young women who find themselves pregnant. The anthropologist made much of her relationship with the young girls she had been interviewing, and so I asked if they had ever intimated that they had experienced any untoward sexual advances or even abuse prior to the pregnancy. She paused, clearly irritated by my difficult question, appeared to search her memory and then said 'yes, on one occasion, a young woman of 14 had said that she thought she had been abused by her uncle' but before I could reply she very quickly said 'but of course I told her that if she wasn't sure then she had better not say anything because it might not be true'. I felt sick.

As I intimated in Chapter 1, there is a whole voiceless group of people who only have researchers to help them tell their stories, and the responsibility for doing this is considerable. This young woman had thought the researcher was genuinely interested in her story, had trusted her and was testing out this trust. I wondered not for the first time how much longer this experience condemned the young woman to silence, as her truth was denied.

Why Are You Talking about It Now?

Excited that I am to deliver my first paper at an international conference, I mention it at the end of a session to a group I am teaching. In a nutshell I try to tell them the gist of my paper and their discussion gives me ideas and support. I'm aware of a brooding silence from one of the mature students who breaks into this informal discussion with a sneer. 'That can't be true' she says in response to my admission of my own abuse, 'why have you waited so long to talk about it?' I feel shocked. 'Are you calling me a liar?' is a question that dangles between us unanswered. This is not the first time I have been challenged and as on previous occasions I have cause to wonder what this woman might reveal of her own experience, just what raw nerve I had touched to invite such a stinging retort.

Silenced by the Editor

Not many days go by without there being some mention of the epidemic of teenage pregnancy in the paper and 20 March 1998 was no exception. There in the correspondence pages of *The Guardian* is a letter from a deputy headmistress called Mary

Crawford (1998, p. 21), who knows that her year 11 girls are producing babies, not 'O' levels, because their mothers are encouraging and colluding with them. My reply is immediate, passionate and with very little hope of publication, but I decide not to withhold my name.

On Monday morning there is my letter under the heading 'Tale of a teenage mother', reproduced as I had written it but with my name withheld (Anon, 1998). I am silenced. Why can the, in my opinion inane, response from a headmistress be included over her signature, and yet mine, outlining an equally serious view, have my name withheld? If the editor was protecting me, what was it from? I feel, not for the first time, the power of the dominant discourse.

We Can't Blame the Parents

I listen to yet another paper at a conference, delivered by someone from a prestigious university who has a large grant to study teenage pregnancy in his area. My hand no longer shoots up to ask questions, I am weary of the same responses, but something about this anthropologist gives me hope. Collaring him during the refreshment break, I tell him I am intrigued by the particular geographical area he is working in and that it has a higher than average teenage pregnancy rate. Isn't it interesting, I say, that in 1987 Dr Marietta Higgs was being castigated for suggesting that this area also had a higher than average sexual abuse rate. Did he think there was any connection? Could it be built into the research design? We exchanged emails for a while, considering the possibilities, then came the inevitable response 'it would be an ethical nightmare to be questioning parents about their behaviour, better to stick to examining the behaviour of the young women who become pregnant'.

Self indulgence

In the light of increased interest in the role of the individual in research I am emboldened to include autoethnography as a research technique in my social sciences module. Intended as a discussion about the contribution of the individual story to research, I expected stimulated discussion. I received some angry, negative, anonymous evaluations, the most stinging of which was that this was sheer 'self indulgence'; the unenlightened responses hurt. I wanted to retaliate but resisted with wise counsel.

FROM INVISIBILITY TO PUBLIC SCRUTINY

These six responses are not exhaustive of the range of responses I have received, however they do highlight particular issues that may impact on you telling your story and for which you need to be prepared, supported and ready to respond. One thing

I have discovered is that if you are prepared to put your story into the public domain the audience, whether it is at a conference, in a classroom, or an anonymous reviewer, will feel that you are capable of tackling quite blatant criticism. It is as if the very nature of your public explanation exonerates you from the respect that might accompany a personal confession. Nowhere was this more obvious than when someone asked me whether, if abortion had been legal when I got pregnant, I would have had my son aborted? This was delivered with the sort of cold, calculating, clinical distance which belied the enormity of the question I was being asked.

The issues to be considered can be focused on the personal level of risk and energy required not only to respond to the challenges that result, but to dealing with the stories of others that your contribution provokes. It is best to keep calm and dignified through the rhetoric and claims of self indulgence. You may well have to respond just as imaginatively to the large questions about truth and memory as to small prurient interest in the detail of your story. Are you ready for your voice to be further silenced by powerful institutions and to have to justify the ethics of engaging in personal stories that may involve others? Are you ready to 'feel the restlessness of history, the transience of culture and the spatial and temporal borders of identity within us' (Spry, 2001, p. 53). If so, then let's start to tease out some of these reactions and find some explanations to defend our right to not be silenced.

REACTIONS TO STORIES

There is a common expression that the truth often hurts. Leaving aside the difficulties of establishing what 'the truth' might be, this phrase usually refers to an individual telling another in very clear terms what they think of some aspect of their behaviour. This may be as simple as telling someone that a certain colour doesn't suit them, or more profoundly why you no longer want a relationship with them. Usually this 'truth' is a one-sided perspective dressed up as doing something for the other person's own good. But these truths are usually no more than perpetuations of dominant discourses about right and wrong behaviour. The hurt felt by the recipient of this 'truth' could be just another bodily expression of the denial of their own truth. In a report entitled 'Truth hurts' (McLoughlin, 2006, p. 508), young people described their experiences of self harm and, over and over again, they said that their experience of asking for help often made their situation worse. They appeared to be hurt by telling the truth of their story as well as embodying this hurt by harming themselves.

LEGITIMACY

Engagement with another's experience then requires imaginative participation, but this still perhaps leaves some important questions unanswered such as, is the story truthful? Is it coherent and, given that many stories are told in retrospect, to what extent does memory play a part in the veracity and accuracy of the story? Does writing a story, even in the present time, ensure that it will be more accurate? Even if I wrote a diary of my experience today, it would be highly selective and may differ from that of my husband with whom I have spent the day. And, if not 'truthful' can a work of fiction give some clues as to the human condition? Other methodologies can fall back on claims of validity and reliability as they struggle to control the variables that make everyday life so complicated, including qualitative researchers who make claims of trustworthiness or veracity.

REFLEXIVITY

Kvale (1996, p. 229) contends that concepts of validity, generalisabilty and reliability in modern social sciences 'have reached the status of a scientific holy trinity'. A criticism often levelled at qualitative research methods is that these issues may be inadequately addressed. However, Horsburgh (2003) argues that such conceptualisations as are used to judge a quantitative approach are wholly unsuitable for evaluating qualitative research. She concludes that criteria used in the evaluation of research must be appropriate for the particular research paradigm in question. Storytelling especially has been condemned as biased, personal, ungeneralisable and unscientific (Koch, 1998). Nevertheless, the intrinsic tenets of the evaluation system remain the same. The researcher's account must be seen to be plausible and trustworthy. Given the embodied nature of many stories, I have come to think of the appropriate criteria for evaluation as akin to the gut reaction, the intuitive response or just an impression of that 'just makes sense to me'. I refer to this response as resonance.

RESONANCE

> Life is a song. It has its own rhythm of harmony.
> It is a symphony of all things which exist in major
> and minor keys of Polarity. It blends all the discords, by opposites
> into a harmony which unites the whole in a grand
> symphony of life. (Sills, 1989, p. x)

I like the metaphor of life as a song, it allows for the resonance of the song to become a response to its qualities, the catchiness of the lyric and the hook of the refrain. Resonance is easily described in musical terms; I only have to listen to the opening chords of The Kinks record 'You Really Got Me' to be transported bodily back to the youth club in the 1960s. It is more than just a memory. I can feel the desperation of my desire to be liked, smell the espresso coffee and hear the whirr and clicks of the jukebox. I can feel the guitar chords echoing deep in my gut as my fingers tap out the rhythm. I remember the words, I can sing along. This music vibrates throughout my body with echoes of my youth. I would suggest that autoethnographic stories can resonate, not just by pulling at the heart strings or provoking memories but by eliciting a response to the text that, as Lacan says, 'surprises the unconscious' (Chaitin, 2008, p. 234).

I am also intrigued by the idea of Songlines, invisible pathways that meander all over Australia and are known to the aboriginals as Footprints of the Ancestors. Aboriginal Creation myths tell of the legendary beings who wander over the continent in Dreamtime, singing out the name of everything that crossed their path and so singing the world into existence (Chatwin, 1998, p. 2). David Carless sings his experience into existence in Chapter 7 and, while the lyrics can also be important, the music taps another layer of consciousness that reverberates in a non-verbal way.

All creation myths are trying to make sense of the truth of our existence and how it came to be, and nearly every writer, philosopher, spiritual leader, scientist social scientist grapples with the concept. In keeping with the sense of an embodied truth, Nietzsche (1989, p. 88) posits that 'All credibility, all good conscience, all evidence of truth come only from the senses'.

ENGAGING WITH THE TEXT – ROLE OF REVIEWER AND READER

As I start to re-write in response to known and unknown reviewers and editors' comments, I am reminded that writing is not a linear process, and what seems like the end is also the beginning. Like all creative work, within whose scope I include research, it is iterative. What you know at the end affects what comes before it, ably described by T.S. Eliot (2001) in the first of his four quartets, 'Burnt Norton':

> Time present and time past /Are both perhaps present in time future,
> And time future contained in time past.

However, most importantly, there is an audience for whom the work is intended. I consider these reviewers as advocates for you, the reader, and set out, as one of my earliest tutors drummed into me, to make further what is implicit explicit. I am delving into the dusty corners of my ideas once again to provide another layer of explanation that appears to be missing in places. One of my implicit assumptions followed the myth that facts speak for themselves. Intuitively I know they don't, but I think my reservation to be more explicit is something to do with maintaining a certain amount of mystery to the process of creating an autoethnography, which is clearly not helpful in a book that sets out to explain the mystery.

I am intrigued by the role of the reviewer in publishing an autoethnographic account. First, given the amount of personal information that is contained in the text and the fairly small world of autoethnographic authors, anonymity in the reviewing process is quite hard to maintain. Also, questions are raised about the reactions of the reviewer. They can share an intuitive response, check for resonance with the piece, and make comments about the aesthetics of the piece; but on many occasions authors have added the reviewer's response into the finished article: Sparkes (1996);

Mykhalovskiy (1996); Holt (2003); and Wall (2006), to name just a few. These reviews are recognised for the contribution they make to the finished piece of work, not so much acting as a gatekeeper to the journal but engaging in dialogue and social reflexivity.

SELF INDULGENCE OR SOMETHING MORE?

Isn't it rather self-indulgent to talk about your self in this way? Isn't it just self promotion, or baring the soul to elicit sympathy? My first response to this is to explain that, like other researchers, the autoethnographer really believes that they have something to contribute to enhance other people's understanding of society. However, if you have ever experienced some of the reactions I have had from audiences, as I have described previously, claims that I am lying or just so different from the norm that my story is irrelevant, you would not subject yourself to this unless there was a strong belief that the purpose was legitimate.

Mykhalovskiy (1996, p. 147) provides an excellent response to the accusations of self indulgence by stating that, far from being a solitary process, writing only for those who produce it, an autoethnography is a social process engaging with a readership, 'a dialogic and collaborative process', with an author prepared to engage with the critical reviewer and the wider social processes. The real test of self indulgence must be: do you, the reader, find anything of value in what has been written?

Sparkes (2002, p. 15) traces the universal charge·of self indulgence in vulnerable writing back to a 'deep mistrust of the worth of the self'. He suggests that autoethnographies can encourage 'acts of witnessing, empathy and connection that extend beyond the self or the author and contribute to sociological understanding in ways that among others are self knowing, self-respectful, self sacrificing and self-luminous' (p. 222).

I can still remember the review of a first draft of a previous text. Encouraged by my co-editor to avoid academic jargon and make the book readable, back came the anonymous review that the text was written in a 'humanistic chatty style'. I was initially horrified; this was my academic reputation at stake. Sensibly, we chose to interpret this review as a compliment: we had written a book that was readable, that could be understood by professional health carer, academic and lay person alike.

COHERENCE

Writers refer to the fragmented and disrupted nature of their story (Sparkes, 2000), and the partial narrative that they offer (Meekums, 2008), so looking for an accurate, composite and complete version is unrealistic. Making judgements about the quality of autoethnographic texts can really only take place through debate and discussion. There is no one easily applied set of criteria for an 'external referent point or a set of facts that exist independently of themselves and their historical conditions' (Sparkes, 2000, p. 37). Perhaps Sparkes's (2000, p. 29) most important reminder about the quality of a piece of writing is 'to use the literary criteria of coherence, verisimilitude and interest'; echoing the general aims of realism in offering 'truthful, accurate and objective representation of the real world, both the external world and the human self' (Habib, 2008, p. 471). This requires strategies that use descriptive and evocative detail but avoid the fantastical, the imaginary and the mythical.

IMAGINATIVE PARTICIPATION

By hurting us with their own perceptions of truth, other people deny us our stories, whether this is the denial of an alternative explanation for our behaviour, or a right to wear clashing colours with pride if we want to. Someone else has to be able to imagine what it is like to be us, and this requires imaginative participation, sometimes called empathy. Hume (2007, p. 419) is the best known proponent of the idea that 'the sentiments of others can never affect us, but by becoming, in some measure our own … these other sentiments are made available to us through an operation of the imagination. Imaginative ability can be the route to others' world of meaning'.

Richard Wollheim (1984) uses the analogy of how an audience may respond to a character in a dramatic performance to contrast the ways that we have of conceiving others' experience. He suggests that there are three ways: detachment, empathy and sympathy. Denham (2000, p. 219) suggests this serves as a good illustration of how subjective imagination can enhance our understanding of others' experiential perspectives 'to grasp the consequences of its truth'. In order to empathise with the experience of another, one needs to 'withhold a judgement of it as true'. Also, the person who can form an imaginative conception of the other's point of view will be better able to elaborate the likely consequences of that other's experiences, as in the example of shared jokes in Chapter 4 (Denham, 2000, p. 219).

So telling a story needs to capture the imagination so that the listener can gain access to the world of meaning of the teller. Telling the truth of one's story then is not for the faint-hearted. There is no doubt that personal stories have started to appear in research, but the world appears to want sanitised 'personal narrative' or 'reflections', lived experiences constrained within the philosophical traditions of Heidegger or Husserl, not a story that doesn't fit with received wisdom, one that is complicated by its gaps and omissions and that is uncomfortable to hear.

INDIVIDUALS IN POPULATIONS

I opened this book with the challenge that lack of mutual understanding was a key problem in the 21st century. Lack of shared understanding permeates political, cultural, artistic and scientific practices. While there is less tolerance for the idea of a grand narrative of historical development or 'a series of archetypes with claims to universal explanatory power' (Habib, 2008, p. 772), interest has grown in more narrowly defined fields and areas of interest. Habib (2008, p. 773) argues that even the pursuit of reality has been reduced to an ideological construct with a return to a 'rhetorical and sceptical vision whereby we recognise not only the constitution of our perceptual and conceptual capacity by language but also the constitutive role of the linguistic situation itself'. He suggests that 'this is fraught with all the multifold dimensions of performance, all of the historically specific circumstances which internally shape the process of communication, whether philosophical, political or literary'.

Autoethnography has to be considered within the period often referred to as the postmodern, where provocative modes of discourse, writing and criticism have led to the abandonment of the search for facts and truths, challenging traditional boundaries between art and science.

TEXT

Postmodern philosophy arose from an attempt to extend the influence of modernism into the areas of language and literature. It was Ferdinand de Saussure (1983) who drew attention to the arbitrary nature of the relationship between the signifier (the word) and the signified (the concept); for example there is no reason why 'cat' should signify a small furry creature. Language has meaning only through a linguistic chain of differentiations. He identified the difference between the system of language ('Langue') and the idiosyncratic speech of individuals ('Parole'), and was first to distinguish between the 'synchronic' study of language (language at a given time), and the 'diachronic' (language as it changes through time).

In this postmodern turn Derrida overturned the Cartesian view of the subject and suggested that difference was at the heart of everything. In his 'decentred' universe devoid of all certainties, Derrida challenged us with the idea that 'there is nothing outside the text' (Derrida, 1967, p. 158), which is taken to mean that everything was a potential subject for analysis by deconstruction. It was Derrida who pushed post-structuralism beyond its origins in the study of literature to become a challenge for science. By 'writing' he meant not just words on a page but 'cinematography, choreography, painting, music sculpture, sport, politics, cybernetics and life itself' (Derrida, 1967, p. 9). Derrida's idea of writing was not to get close to a single truth but to challenge that very idea. 'We do not read in order to discover the truth; reading is the starting point for our own writing; our own construction of our own text' (Rolfe, 2000, p. 40).

Lyotard (1979) eventually formalised Derrida's work and employed the term post-modernism in a philosophical sense. An important aspect of what he considered to be 'real' postmodernism as opposed to the anything goes message of deconstructionism, was the question of legitimation of knowledge. Not what is real or not, or what counts as knowledge or what doesn't, but how those decisions are made and who makes them. This is what Foucault (1980) described as the 'general politics' of truth or the types of discourses society accepts and makes function as if it were true, to which Lyotard added 'knowledge and power are simply two sides of the same question: who decides what knowledge is, and who knows what needs to be decided?' (Lyotard, 1982, pp. 8–9).

A great deal of what we learn about the world is through the written word. Everything from comics to newspapers, from novels and autobiographies to research texts can only be understood through language, and the weight of historical thinking that engulfs you as you dip into the text. Even the globalising impact of the internet depends on the ability to read to engage with it. However, it is not feasible to have read everything on a subject in order to engage in a dialogue; and it is certainly not necessary to have read everything to form an opinion about something.

In his book 'How to talk about books you haven't read', Bayard (2008) reminds us that while we have an obligation to read and read thoroughly, and that we should ideally have read a book thoroughly, to be able to talk about it, it is entirely possible to talk about a book that we haven't read. It occurs to me that talking about texts we haven't read underpins a great deal of academic writing – skim reading texts for a quote, reading reviews of work instead of the text itself, are shortcuts to the sheer volume of work that it might be necessary for you to know. Literature reviews are the ultimate short cut, selecting only a small section of literature to underpin a further research study and conveying a sense of the landscape of the research arena as an intellectual exercise rather than a thorough review.

What is not acknowledged is the huge variety of influences that come to permeate that selection, the whole journey of experience through education, family values, employment, reading, travel ... the list is endless. These experiences also encompass our cultural heritage, which has filtered down through myth and folklore into our everyday lives without having engaged with any text at all. All these experiences bring you, the reader, to a particular point in time and underpin your understanding of the current text. This accumulation of experience and reading is eventually absorbed and embodied, and becomes readily available as common sense.

COMMON SENSE

Even the ideas that we think of as common sense can be traced back to some historical precedent which then becomes read through a modern lens and reinterpreted on the street. A good example of this is the whole history of what it is to be a good parent. With all the assumptions of naturalness, most people who attempt to parent are influenced by at least 200 years of experts' advice with their associated thousands of years of philosophical background. The evidence is often started by politically motivated writing and research with a firm footing in religious practices, stirred and shaken by psychologists and sociologists, which is then interpreted and reinterpreted by books, magazines and soap operas until it takes on the hue of obviousness and naturalness by the population as a whole. Within this *mêlée* of ideas and practices the experiences of individuals become swamped by generalisations. It may seem 'obvious' from the psychological and sociological literature that children need fathers, despite the widespread knowledge that abused children are often abused by members of their own family; but this obviousness has to be countered by the political imperative that families should be funded by parents, with the state providing backup only where absolutely necessary. Fathers are an economic necessity as much as a psychological support, but it suits the government that psychodynamics has become the metaphor for all parenting, with a pervasiveness that defies its intellectual origins.

Individuals populate this research but their invisibility means they have no voice. When we talk about research findings, we are talking mostly about people who are unheard and silenced by the power and control of the researcher in their efforts to provide generalisable findings.

SCIENCE AS MYTH

Within the myths that surround science is the idea of the self as a contaminant in research, and this supports one of the dominant criticisms of autoethnography. The pervasive view of even qualitative research is that there is an objective truth that can be found, and that to do this requires moving many complex variables and subjectivity from the process. However, science itself cannot be removed from the world in which it is conducted and it is important to recognise that scientific metaphors do not constitute empirical reality; that they may obscure as well as illuminate. Research is just one story among many others that can be illustrated in the myths that underpin our culture.

In her consideration of the rise of fundamentalism in religion, Armstrong (2001) suggests that the mythical underpinnings of our culture, what the Greeks called Mythos, are now ignored in favour of rational, pragmatic scientific thought, or Logos, despite the need for for society both to function and to remain in balance. This same fundamentalism can be seen in research, particularly in healthcare. Myths are about the unknown, stories that help us find our place in the world, explaining the sublime and that there's more to life than meets the eye, with even science being considered a myth. At their best, myths and stories can teach us compassion and make us live more fully. But just as myths and stories are lost in the wider world of research, the world of research contains many missing stories.

Roland Barthes (1993) analysed contemporary French culture in a series of essays, which he collectively called 'Mythologies', in which he advises that we should be cautious about myths, as they conceal political motives, and circulate ideology through society. Acknowledging her indebtedness to Barthes, Warner (1994, p. xiii) criticises Barthes's fundamental principle that 'myths are not eternal verities, but historical compounds, which successfully conceal their own contingency, changes and transitoriness so that the story they tell looks as if it cannot be told otherwise' and 'that things always were like that and always shall be'. Warner is less pessimistic; she believes that the process of understanding and clarification can lead to the continuous process of weaving new stories into the social fabric.

Rituals have deep connections with myth. They serve to tie people into patterns of experience that don't require individual thought, while receiving external validation. As a young student nurse, I can remember being in awe of the 'expertise' of my senior nursing colleagues, who knew exactly what patients needed and when. As I learned by rote the practices of post-operative care, I didn't really stop to think whether sips of fluid were really required within one hour of return to the ward from theatre, or suppositories within 48 hours. The care worked like clockwork, patients recovered and complaints were rare. Nursing care was something we did to patients: we thought *for* them, not in consultation with them. Research sometimes seems like this. Research is done using individuals rather than in consultation with them.

It could be argued that we are no closer to understanding individuals despite decades of research. Education still fails some children; healthcare still fails to help many patients. Many of the major challenges facing society depend on improving understanding of why people behave as they do and how to maximise the effectiveness with which individuals can take control of their own lives.

MIXING ART AND SCIENCE, ILLUSIONS AND REALITIES

The distinction between illusion (with its connotations of fallacy and self deception) and reality had a kind of watershed in the late 19th and 20th centuries. After 500 years of artistic striving for visual accuracy, with considerable accomplishment in illusionistic technique, and following the advent of the photographic camera, artists and critics began to question whether or not, since the beginning of the Renaissance, things had stood on their heads, and that 'reality' had at least as much, and possibly more, to do with what was known to exist in external nature than with what one saw. Reality was as much a quality of mind as it was of matter.

> For the scientist, both the universe and his theory of it are beautiful, in much the same sense that a work of art can be regarded as beautiful ... Of course the scientist and the artist differ in a very important respect. For the scientist works mainly at the level of very abstract ideas, while his perceptual contact with the world is largely mediated by instruments. On the other hand, the artist works mainly on creating concrete objects that are directly perceptible without instruments. Yet as one approaches the broadest possible field of science, one discovers closely related criteria of 'truth' and 'beauty'. For what the artist creates must be 'true to itself', just as the broad scientific theory must be 'true to itself' ... (t)he artist really needs a scientific attitude to his work, as the scientist must have an artistic attitude to his. (Bohm, 2004, pp. 22–3)

Since the time of Plato, philosophical thinking had a tendency towards finding universality, reaching a climax in the Middle Ages when theology was at the apex of the intellectual hierarchies. Humanity was conceived as having an appointed place and all dimensions; bodily, emotional, intellectual and spiritual had a defined location in the universe. More recently, this idea of a coherent view of the world has dissolved, hastened by changes in political and economic development. Gradual preoccupation with the particular and the local in research as well as in mass culture is the product of a long historical development. Somewhere in this development the separation of aesthetic and rationality occurred. Any thinker, writer or critic before the end of the 18th century would have been puzzled to find a distinction being made between 'literature' and the political, moral and educational fields of 'science'. The distinction has its roots in the Enlightenment.

The Enlightenment is often referred to in reductive fashion as the age of reason; however, this fails to consider the intellectual trends of the period. Enlightenment thinkers ushered in an 'era of humanitarian, intellectual and social progress underlain by the increasing ability of human reason to subjugate analytically both the external world of nature and the human self' (Habib, 2008, p. 311).

Some researchers are using creative methods to discover academic legitimacy in the nexus between art and science; sometimes individuals, sometimes a discipline such as Arts Based Educational Research (Barone and Eisner, 2006). The epistemic and aesthetic demands of autoethnography in particular attempt to subvert dominant cultural discourses and add performance as an alternative to textual practice. The separation of art and science can be found in Locke's philosophy, which laid the foundations of classical British empiricism. His work is often characterised as marked by tolerance, moderation and common sense, and it supports many of the ideological forces present today. He read Descartes, was a friend of Newton and was heavily influenced by the experimental methods of Sir Robert Boyle. The implications of his work still resonate, underpinning the forces that encourage us to look at the world as a set of facts, which our minds then process, to give us a set of abstract ideas and general truths. Locke's views about language are particularly interesting, providing as they did the starting point for theories about language in the 18th century and anticipating the advance of modern literary criticism. Locke believed language to be closely associated with the process of thought. He revived the age-old antagonism between philosophy on the one side and rhetoric on the other. 'All the artificial and figurative applications of Words Eloquence hath invented are for nothing else but to insinuate wrong Ideas, move the passions and thereby mislead the Judgment' (cited in Nidditch, 1975, p. 508).

Whereas the Renaissance had done much to integrate human pursuits and faculties, Locke wanted a clear separation.

FALSE DICHOTOMY

Macy (2000, p. 133) defines the conventional notion of the self as

> the metaphoric construct of identity and agency, the hypothetical piece of turf on which we construct our strategies for survival, the notion around which we focus our instincts for self preservation, our needs for self-approval, and the boundaries of our self-interest.

This view of subjectivity implies that everybody has a different world view that somehow we can separate ourselves from 'out there' and produce a view that is distinct from the objective world of science. Rose (1991) argues in *Governing the Soul* that the autonomy of self is a delusion, with subjectivity just as controlled by experts. While citizens of liberal democracies appear to shape their lives, 'it is possible to govern subjectivity according to norms and criteria that ground their authority in an esoteric but objective knowledge' (Rose, 1991, p. 9). He insists that 'we live under the beguiling illusion that our subjective lives are a personal matter'. He argues that our intimate lives, our feelings, desires and aspirations, while seeming quintessentially personal, are in fact social, organised and managed in minute detail in three ways.

- The personal and subjective capacities have been incorporated into the scope and aspirations of public powers, e.g. family obligations, child welfare, surveillance of parents.
- The management of subjectivity has become a central task for the modern organisation: increased productivity requires consideration of group dynamics.
- There is an expertise of subjectivity, 'engineers of the soul' who have a profound effect in the relations of authority over the self.

It is it virtually impossible to say where the objective world stops and the subjective view begins. How autonomous is our sense of self, how free are we to think the way we do? Is our soul governed by the state or is it a free spirit to toss and turn on the tide of our own destiny? Is it free and shapeless or has it quietly become engineered and controlled?

Into this mêlée of subjectivity and objectivity comes a desire by some to reflect a human science, one that recognises the constraints and limitations of boundaries but privileges the stories of individuals who wish to shed light on various aspects of human behaviour. Instead of explanation and the establishment of general laws to understand people, Romanyshyn (1982, p. 89) emphasises 'imaginal reconstruction'. The psychologist's task is to deepen our imagination. We understand another when we can imagine him or her. To imagine or make sense of another or ourselves, we weave a story.

TRUTH

In all research, validity or 'truth' of findings is paramount; but how to determine truth? A positivist belief in an objective world where knowledge reflects reality (Kvale, 1996) is at odds with the postmodern concept where 'truth' is regarded as socially constructed. Truth in the postmodern world allows all viewpoints to be heard with no one view held as an absolute truth. As Cheek (2000, p. 20) points out 'post-modern thought emphasizes that reality is plural and that there are multiple positions from which it is possible to view any aspect of reality'. Thus Guba and Lincoln (1994) argue that delivery of the definitive truth is an impossible task for one single research method. Derrida (1976, p. 158) proclaimed that 'there is nothing outside, or beyond, the text'; the whole world is a potential subject for analysis by deconstruction. His idea was not to narrow down towards a single truth but rather a broadening out towards multiple truths. Lyotard (1984) suggested that 'real' postmodernism is more to do with the legitimation of knowledge, and not a question of what is real and what is not, or even what counts as knowledge and what does not, but rather of how those decisions are made and who makes them. Lyotard claims that we have now lost the ability to believe in meta-narratives.

The question then becomes, what now forms the basis of legitimation in society if there is no overarching meta-narrative? For Lyotard, the answer lies in the philosophy of Wittgenstein. If we have rejected grand narratives, then what we have fallen back on are little narratives. Therefore, what legitimates knowledge in the postmodern condition is how well it performs, or how it enables a person to perform, each little story.

BAKHTIN

Bakhtin gives me a satisfactory definition of truth:

> 'Language lives' says Bakhtin 'only in the dialogic interaction of those who make it. It is an unfortunate misunderstanding (a legacy of rationalism) to think that truth can only be the truth that is composed of universal moments; that the truth of a situation is precisely that which is repeatable and constant in its use'. (Cited in Shotter and Billig, 1998, p. 13)

Bakhtin attempts to reconcile the false dichotomy between objectivism and subjectivism. Bakhtin regards 'truth' as something that is constituted dialogically and intersubjectively, that reason is not the only way to truth; it is constituted through conversation (Bell and Gardiner, 1998). Bakhtin also gives me a justification for using personal stories in the world of 'research'; he suggests we analyse or understand events in terms of what makes them creative, singular or contingent, and the most important aspect for him is to understand an act's relation to other acts, ethics and history, and that remembering is a social rather than an individual activity (Bell and Gardiner, 1998).

One of Bakhtin's key concepts was Prosaics, a mechanism for exploring 'the chaos of lived experience' (Holquist, 2002, p. 31). Exploring the humanities, Morson (2003, p. 378) suggests that Prosaics is a way of thinking about the 'ordinary, messy, quotidian facts of daily life as opposed to the grand, dramatic or catastrophic'. He suggests that this is an attempt to reconcile what he describes as the two entrenched positions of the schools of thought in the humanities.

> On the one hand is 'semiotic totalitarianism', where proponents assume that to understand any part of culture, one must first devise a system capable of explaining every part of it; and on the other hand are the 'village relativists' who 'detect metaphysical and epistemological errors in their adversaries' thought', repeatedly find new ways to conclude that one can't know anything with certainty and therefore, completely illogically, that one can't know anything at all. (Morson, 2003, pp. 377–8)

At the end of the chapter, Morson (2003, p. 389) reminds us that reading is a series of small decisions and moment to moment judgements, and this process is the point of his book: 'Like true life, art begins where the tiny bit begins'.

One only has to spend some time reminiscing with a family member about a shared event to know that shared memories do not uncover a verifiable truth. Spence reminds us that 'narrative truth is not a substitute for historical truth' (1982, pp. 97, 94). Historical truth refers to events that occurred in the remembered past; narrative truth refers to events that either may or may not have actually happened in the historical past but are believed to be true (in the psychological sense) by the rememberer. Does disagreeing about details of the event necessarily negate your memory?

FALSE MEMORY SYNDROME

Memories of abuse have become inextricably linked to false memory syndrome (FMS). The attempts to deny my story give me further cause to reflect on how many other truths are denied. This presents a recurring philosophical idea in my patchwork life, namely, what is truth? Whose truth is valuable? Can truth vary? Is an experience true if it corresponds with the facts, or is there an absolute truth that depends on the consistency of the whole? Research has never been very successful in accepting new ideas that don't conform to received wisdom, hence the proliferation of theory to support FMS (Loftus, 1993; Loftus et al., 1994). Rather than accept the harsh reality that some women damaged by sexual abuse may be telling the truth, FMS conveys a powerful expert voice to silence the weakened victim.

Polusny and Follette (1996) reported that there are two consequences of FMS. First, the majority of psychologists focus on the possibility that clients report abuse before therapy; and second, that of unscientific intolerance: namely, if you hold a different view, your book should be banned.

MEMORY

There is no doubt that memory is a key feature of autobiographical accounts, and in fact autobiographical memory is a particular feature of memory research. Implicit in the early research around memory is that if recall is accurate, a truth can be found that can be verified against external sources. Historically psychological studies of memory have fallen mainly into two camps. One camp represents those who have attempted to remove meaning from the study in order to devise models of how memory might work, producing the familiar Short-Term Memory, Long-Term Memory and Working memory. In the other camp are others who place meaning as a central feature of the study of memory, such as Bartlett's (1932) classic study 'The War of the Worlds'.

Neisser (1976) believed that the important questions that arise out of memory are those that arise out of everyday experience, by which he meant naturally occurring behaviour in the natural context of the real world. He referred to the idea of ecological validity, wherein the conditions of any experiment should represent real world phenomena. For Neisser, memory in general does not exist, it is a left-over concept from medieval psychology. He called on theories of memory to reflect human experience. Particularly important is the use of memory for using past experience to explore the present and the future.

Memories are a construction or, perhaps more accurately, a reconstruction of past events in the present, whether the remembrances are of mundane daily activities or of anomalous, life altering events. Memory traces are like books that must be purchased and catalogued; the prospective user must look up the book in the catalogue to know where to find it. For the search to succeed it must not have been eaten by worms or misplaced by a careless user.

MEMORY METAPHOR

Metaphors figure prominently in memory research. Payne and Blackwell (1998, p. 38) describe a long list of spatial analogies used to explain human memory. They range from the well-known Wax tablet (Plato, Aristotle) and Library (Broadbent) and Tape Recorder (Posner and Warren), to the bizarre Cow's stomach (Hintzman) and Garbage can (Landauer). I particularly like the Rooms in a house (Freud). Houses are full of memories and ghosts that fit well with autobiographical writing. But these are all trying to explain forgetting rather than how ideas are retained. What are the effects of memory metaphors? If they are likened to physical objects deposited in a space of some kind, the following questions are likely to need to be addressed. What factors affect the ease of locating an item in memory? What makes a retrieval cue effective in helping us to recover a memory? How does our ability to retrieve information change across the retention interval?

EXHUMED MEMORY

The library metaphor takes us a long way, but the notion of memory retrieval obscures the fact that memories can be distorted, biased and otherwise altered by changes in perspective and by other events that occur after the time of encoding. This is particularly evident in the considerable inaccuracies reported by Loftus (1979) in accounts of eyewitness testimony, where even witnesses present at the scene of accidents can recall entirely different perspectives of the event they witnessed. Many aspects of our lives depend on our beliefs about the functioning of our memory. Payne and Blackwell note that half the states in the United States changed their statute of limitations for filing charges based on 'recovered memories', which they say speaks volumes for the impact that beliefs about memory have on society (Payne and Blackwell, 1998, p. 33).

But for its slightly sinister overtones, I think Kihlstrom's (1998, p. 12) idea of exhumed memory is particularly pertinent to the role of memory in recall of autoethnographic accounts connected to memories of trauma and deprivation in childhood. He is referring to the 'exhumation of repressed or perhaps dissociated memories' and suggests that memory is not analogous to reading a book, it is more like writing a book from fragmentary notes' (p. 18), highlighting the principle of memory reconstruction.

This of course raised concerns about the extent to which memories are accurate. Are certain memories more accurate than others? Are there important differences in the quantity, quality and accuracy of memories across the lifespan? Can certain memories, including traumatic ones, be forgotten or repressed for long periods only to resurface, with force and feeling, many years later in psychotherapy and other situations? Are some procedures more helpful than others in obtaining accurate memories?

CONCLUSIONS DRAWN FROM MEMORY RESEARCH

It is quite clear that accurate and permanent retention are not features of human memory. Lakoff and Johnson (1980) suggest we mis-remember the details of events, and 'remember' events that did not occur. Episodic memory refers to the recall of certain events, and this has demonstrated the flaws in the container approach to how memories work. One of the popular ways of testing episodic memory is to ask someone to recall what they were doing on the occasion of a public event. I learnt the importance of context in this exercise when I asked my psychology students to recall what they were doing when man first landed on the moon. I had judged that they were not old enough to recall the death of John Kennedy, or of England winning the World Cup, but even the moon landing was a historical event for all but one of the students, who was in nursery school at the time.

A recent memorable event was the death of Princess Diana. I remember vividly sitting in my car with my daughter as a passenger at some traffic lights in my village at exactly 8 am, when just before the news, they played the national anthem. Not being a regular listener to radio on a Sunday morning, I had no idea whether or not this was a common event. The reason I remember this so vividly is because this was my only experience of attending a car-boot sale. However, no matter how vivid the event, I do not recall what I was wearing that day or what I ate or even what the weather was like; just the bare bones of this unique occasion.

REMEMBERING

A more helpful way to consider recounting of experiences is in the act of remembering. 'War of the Ghosts', a story read to students in Cambridge in 1932, attempts to recall the story over periods varying from 15 minutes to ten years. Details were forgotten, details added or altered, and these altered details often seemed to match the subject's personal experiences. Bartlett (1932) concluded in his classic monograph *Remembering* that recollection begins with an attitude around which the memory is reconstructed. Therefore attitudes may change over time, affecting the memory. Popular culture now embraces child abuse as a widespread fact of life which will certainly impact on current memories.

There is a 'virtual consensus among memory researchers today that memory is not a complete static and accurate record of the past. Rather, it is a dynamic medium of experience – shaped by expectancies, needs, and beliefs, imbued with emotion, and enriched by the inherently human capacity for narrative creation' (Lynn and Payne, 1997, p. 55).

WHAT MEMORY RESEARCH LEAVES OUT

Memory is a hypothetical construct around which powerful models have been erected and tested. However, models tend to assume that all memory is in the mind and this ignores other senses and bodily reactions. Sparkes reminds us of the challenges and possibilities of using all the senses in our ethnographies, and particularly urges the representation of stories to include particularly smell, touch, taste and hearing, as the visual tends to be over-produced. The notion of acoustic memory is epitomised in a story by Alan Bennett (2005). When talking of his memories of the lady who lived in a van on his driveway for many years, he says it wasn't the squeak of the gate but the door of a broken down van that evoked the strongest memories of her.

I am also reminded of Chopra's ideas of the intelligence within each cell, a knowing beyond scientific reason, that directs the body to heal itself (Chopra, 1990). This excerpt from Bryson (2004, p. 450), called 'Cells', reminds us of the body's fantastic memory that operates with no conscious thought at all.

> Every one of your cells knows exactly what to do to preserve and nurture you from the moment of conception to your last breath. You have no secrets from your cells they know far more about you than you do. Each one carries a copy of the complete genetic code – the instruction manual for the body – so it knows how to do not only its own job but every other job in the body too. Never in your life will you have to remind a cell to keep an eye on its adenosine triphosphate levels or to find a place for the extra squirt of folic acid that's just turned up. It will do that for you and millions of things besides.

And last but by no means the final word on the subject, in true Madame Défarge (Dickens, 2007 [1859]) style, I can still conjure up the trauma of a relationship break-up that I literally knitted into my Autumn Leaves jacket. The symbolism of this is not lost on me: as Madame Défarge knits, her knitting secretly encodes the names of those people she will have killed, symbolising one of the fates whereby life is ended by the cutting of the thread, just as my jacket became synonmous with the ending of a relationship.

ETHICS

Arthur Frank reminds us that ethics of narrative and storytelling is not simply about 'obtaining people's consent to have their story recorded and analyzed' but 'a consideration of the *respect* for stories'. He says that rather than

> bemoan the low condition of story telling in the 'interview society', researchers can lead the process of story telling toward something better. People are not going to stop telling stories; moral life, for better or worse takes place in story telling. Narrative analysis can be a significant model for society that will continue to work out its moral dilemmas in story form. (Frank, 2002, p. 7)

All research requires that the researcher will do no harm to the participants in their studies, so it is interesting to consider who can be harmed by the autoethnographic piece. In it the author is exposed for scrutiny; what risk can they be to themselves or the academy? First, it is important to remember, as stated before in the preface, that none of us lives in a vacuum. Wall (2008, p. 49) highlights her anxiety in being unable to protect the anonymity of her child in her adoption stories, but recognises that using a pseudonym creates an inauthentic and false illusion of protection. Adams (2008, p. 188) presents an excellent overview of narrative ethics in his review from which he proposes three interrelated ethical responsibilities that both authors and readers must continually renegotiate:

> **Acknowledgment of narrative privilege:** Why is an author able to write a life text? How might an author's identities promote ethical blindness? Is the textual playing field equal? Does an author need help crafting her or his stories? What audiences are able to access an author's work?

> **Acknowledgment of (narrative) media:** Where will a narrative appear? How do storying and genre conventions affect a person's story? Who is (un)able to engage with a particular medium? Who develops a medium's conventions and whose interests do these conventions serve?

> **Acknowledgment of ethical violence:** What do you require of a life writer? What do you require of an audience? How might an author's interpersonal obligations affect her or his work? Are you evaluating a text via deductive or inductive criteria?

Bruni (2002, p. 24) suggests that ultimately the responsibility for what is ethical must rest with the researcher, with which I agree; but I don't agree that the diversity of social conditions is avoided due to 'legal, economic and social imperatives', creating a crisis of invisibility. I believe that publishers and ethical committees take it upon themselves to create a protection where it isn't always warranted. I refer to my experience of having a letter published anonymously, when this was not requested, and the stipulation of my first account being anonymised as a case study. However, I would advise, as she does, that the vulnerable researcher provides themselves with appropriate support mechanisms.

TRUTH AND STORY

Truth and story are honourable companions. Diane Setterfield (2006) sums up this relationship in her novel *The Thirteenth Tale*, where she describes the wishes of a dying novelist to at last impart the real story of her existence to a biographer of her choosing. This fascinating story about the concept of truth within a novel epitomises the relationship between truth and story.

> 'I've nothing against people who love truth, she says, apart from the fact that they make dull companions. My gripe is not with lovers of the truth but with truth herself. What succour, what consolation is there in truth, compared to a story?' ... What you need are the plump comforts of a story. (Setterfield, 2006, p. 5)

Summary

- Producing text for an audience will always invite critical review.
- Methodological issues to be dealt with include the legitimacy of this approach and the sub-headings of truth, memory, self indulgence.
- Personal issues to be dealt with include self preservation, hurtful reviews and retorts of lying.
- Resonance is an appropriate criterion for evaluation and this can only be achieved by connecting with the audience through reading, performance or critical review.
- Reviewers can become part of the text, just as supervisors write themselves into every thesis, albeit often quite silently.
- Imaginative ability can be the route to others' world of meaning.
- The self as contaminant is a myth that pervades science.
- Common sense is an illusion with reality, as much a quality of mind as it is of matter; self indulgence or something more.
- Autoethnography requires strategies that use descriptive and evocative detail.
- Coherence, verisimilitude and interest are literary devices for judging the quality of a piece of writing.
- In consideration of the legitimation of knowledge it is not what is true or not true, but how decisions are made and who makes them.
- The analysis and interpretation of autoethnographic texts require the reader to utilise a broader range of analytical skills than those used for other research methods, such as linguistic, semantic and aesthetic analysis and literary criticism.
- Memory is not a complete, static and accurate record of the past. It is dynamic and shaped by expectancies, needs and beliefs, imbued with emotion, and enriched by the inherently human capacity for narrative creation.

- Memory is not all in the mind. Embodiment refers to the absorption of traces of experience throughout the body.
- Ethics is a continually negotiable set of responsibilities between the author and the story and the author and the reader.

FURTHER READING

Mykhalovskiy, E. (1996) Reconsidering table talk: Critical thoughts on the relationship between sociology, autobiography and self-indulgence. *Qualitative Sociology,* **19**(1), 131.

Eric draws attention to the personal costs that attend writing about oneself and suggests that calling an autoethnography self-indulgent is to ignore 'the social relations of readership, content and authorship that the charge of self-involvement invokes' (p. 133). He suggests that there is a specific difference between the solitary writer and the self-indulgent writer in that the latter 'obscures the collective process through which texts of autobiographical sociology are written' (p. 133).

Sparkes, A.C. (2002) Autoethnography: Self indulgence or something more? In A. Bochner and C. Ellis (Eds) *Ethographically Speaking: Autoethnography, literature and aesthetics.* Alta Mira Press, New York.

Andrew uses an autoethnographic account of an accusation of self indulgence to explore a closely argued case that it is so much more. He echoes Bernstein's idea that we have an ethical imperative to 'understand and engage with the incommensurable otherness of the Other' (Bernstein, 1991, p. 66) and to learn to judge differently and listen carefully in research traditions different from our own.

REFERENCES

Adams, T.E. (2008) A review of narrative ethics. *Qualitative Inquiry,* **14**(2), 175–94.

Anon. (1998) Tale of a teenage mother. *The Guardian,* 23 March, p. 17.

Armstrong, K. (2001) *The Battle for God. Fundamentalism in Judaism, Christianity and Islam.* Harper Collins, London.

Barone, T. and Eisner, E. (2006) Arts-based Educational Research. In J. Green, G. Camili and P. Elmore (Eds) *Complementary Methods for Research in Education* (3rd edn). American Educational Research Association, Washington DC.

Barthes, R. (1993) *Mythologies* (trans. A. Lavers). Vintage, London.

Bartlett, F. (1932) *Remembering: A study in experimental and social psychology.* Cambridge University Press, Cambridge.

Bayard, P. (2008) *How to Talk about Books You Haven't Read* (trans. J. Mehlman). Granta Books, London.

Bell, M.M. and Gardiner, M. (Eds) (1998) *Bakhtin and the Human Sciences.* Sage Publications, London.

Bennett, A. (2005) *Untold Stories.* Faber and Faber, London.

Bernstein, R. (1991) *The New Constellation: The ethical–political horizons of modernity/ postmodernity.* Polity Press, Cambridge.

Bohm, D. (2004) *On Creativity.* Routledge, Oxford.

Bruni, N. (2002) The crisis of visibility: Ethical dilemmas of autoethnographic research. *Qualitative Research Journal,* **2**(1), 24–33.

Bryson, B. (2004) *A Short History of Nearly Everything.* Black Swan Books, London.

Chaitin, G.D. (2008) *Rhetoric and Culture in Lacan.* Cambridge University Press, Cambridge.

Chatwin, B. (1998) *The Songlines.* Vintage, London.

Cheek, J. (2000) *Postmodern and Poststructural Approaches to Nursing Research.* Sage, London.

Chopra, D. (1990) *Quantum Healing: Exploring the frontiers of mind body medicine.* Bantum Books, New York.

Cran, A. and Robertson, J. (1996) *Dictionary of Scottish Quotations.* Mainstream, Edinburgh.

Crawford, M. (1998) Why teenage parents are about low expectations. *The Guardian,* 20 March, p. 21.

de Saussure, F. (1983) *Course in General Linguistics (1916).* Duckworth, London.

Denham, A. (2000) *Metaphor and Moral Experience.* Clarendon Press, Oxford.

Derrida, J. (1967 [1974]) *Of Grammatology* (trans. G. Spivak). Johns Hopkins University Press, Baltimore, MD.

Derrida, J. (1976) The End of the Book and the Beginning of Writing (trans. G.C. Spivak). In *Of Grammatology.* Chicago University Press, Chicago.

Dickens, C. (2007 [1859]) *A Tale of Two Cities.* Penguin Classics, London.

Eliot, T.S. (2001) *Four Quartets* (new edn). Faber and Faber, London.

Foucault, M. (1980) *Power/Knowledge: Selected interviews and other writings 1972–77* (trans. C. Gordon, L. Marshall, J. Mepham and K. Soper). Pantheon, New York.

Frank, A.W. (2002) Why study people's stories? The dialogical ethics of narrative analysis. *International journal of Qualitative Methods.* Retrieved 17 December 2007, from http:// www.ualberta.ca/~ijqm

Guba, E.G. and Lincoln, Y.S. (1994) Competing Paradigms in Qualitative Research. In N.K. Denzin and Y.S. Lincoln (Eds) *Handbook of Qualitative Research,* pp. 105–117. Sage, Thousand Oaks, CA.

Habib, M.A.R. (2008) *A History of Literary Criticism and Theory: From Plato to the present.* Blackwell Publishing, London.

Holquist, M. (2002) *Dialogism* (2nd edn). Routledge, London.

Holt, N.L. (2003) Representation, legitimation, and autoethnography: An autoethnographic writing story. *International Journal of Qualitative Methods,* **2**(1), 1.

Horsburgh, D. (2003) Evaluation of qualitative research. *Journal of Clinical Nursing,* **12**(2), 307–12.

Hume, D. (2007) *A Treatise of Human Nature.* New Vision Publications, Sioux Falls, SD.

Kihlstrom, J. (1998) Exhumed Memory. In S. Lynn and K. McConkey (Eds) *Truth in Memory.* Guilford Press, London.

Koch, T. (1998) Story telling: Is it really research? *Journal of Advanced Nursing,* **28**(6), 1182–90.

Kvale, S. (1996) *An Introduction to Qualitative Research Interviewing.* Sage, Thousand Oaks, CA.

Lakoff, G. and Johnson, M. (1980) *Metaphors We Live by.* University of Chicago Press, Chicago, IL.

Loftus, E. (1979) *Eye Witness Testimony*. Harvard University Press, Cambridge, MA.

Loftus, E.F. (1993) The reality of repressed memories. *American Psychologist*, **48**, 518–37.

Loftus, E.F., Polonsky, S. and Fullilove, M.T. (1994) Memories of childhood sexual abuse – remembering and repressing. *Psychology of Women Quarterly*, **18**(1), 67–84.

Lynn, S. and Payne, D. (1997) Memory as the theater of the past: The psychology of false memories. *Current Directions*, **6**, 55.

Lyotard, J-F. (1979[1984]) *The Postmodern Condition: A report on knowledge*. Manchester University Press, Manchester.

Lyotard, J-F. (1982) *The Postmodern Explained to Children*. Turnaround, London.

McLoughlin, C. (2006) Truth hurts: Young people and self harm – a national inquiry. Retrieved October 2008, from http://www.selfharmuk.org/

Macy, J. (2000) Greening the Self – A Buddhist approach. In W. Bloom (Ed.) *Holistic Revolution: The essential new age reader*. Penguin Press, London.

Meekums, B. (2008) Embodied narratives in becoming a counselling trainer: An autoethnographic study. *British Journal of Guidance and Counselling*, **36**(3), 287–301.

Morson, G.S. (2003) Prosaics: An approach to the humanities. In M.E. Gardiner (Ed.) *Mikhail Bakhtin* (Vol. II). Sage, London.

Mykhalovskiy, E. (1996) Reconsidering table talk: Critical thoughts on the relationship between sociology, autobiography and self-indulgence. *Qualitative Sociology*, **19**(1), 131–51.

Neisser, U. (1976) *Cognition and Reality*. Freeman, San Francisco, CA.

Nidditch, P. (Ed.) (1975) *John Locke: An essay concerning human understanding*. Clarendon Press, Oxford.

Nietzsche, F. (1989) *Beyond Good and Evil* (trans. W. Kaufman). Random House, New York.

Payne, D.G. and Blackwell, J.M. (1998) Truth in Memory: Caveat emptor. In S. Lynn and K. McConkey (Eds) *Truth in Memory*. Guilford Press, London, ch. 2.

Polusny, M. and Follette, V. (1996) Remembering childhood sexual abuse: A national survey of psychologists, clinical practice, beliefs, and personal experiences. *Journal of Professional Psychology*, **27**, 41–52.

Rolfe, G. (2000) *Research, Truth, Authority: Postmodern perspectives on nursing*. Macmillan, Basingstoke.

Romanyshyn, R. (1982) *Psychological Life: From science to metaphor*. Open University Press, Milton Keynes.

Rose, N. (1991) *Governing the Soul: The shaping of the private self*. Routledge, London.

Setterfield, D. (2006) *The Thirteenth Tale*. Orion Publishing, London.

Shotter, J. and Billig, M. (1998) A Bakhtinian Psychology: From out of the heads of individuals and into the dialogues between them. In M.M. Bell and M. Gardiner (Eds) *Bakhtin and the Human Sciences*. Sage, London.

Sills, F. (1989) *The Polarity Process*. Element Books, Shaftesbury.

Sparkes, A.C. (1996) The fatal flaw: A narrative of the fragile body-self. *Qualitative Inquiry*, **2**, 463–93.

Sparkes, A.C. (2000) Autoethnography and narratives of self: Reflections on criteria in action. *Sociology of Sport Journal*, **17**(1), 21–43.

Sparkes, A.C. (2002) Autoethnography: Self indulgence or something more? In A. Bochner and C. Ellis (Eds) *Ethographically Speaking: Autoethnography, literature and aesthetics*. Alta Mira Press, New York.

Spence, D. (1982) *Narrative Truth and Historical Truth*. New York: Newton.

Spry, T. (2001) 'From Goldilocks to Dreadlocks: Hair-raising tales of racializing bodies', paper presented at the The Green Window: Giant City Conference on Performative Writing, Southern Illinois University, Carbondale, IL, April.

Wall, S. (2006) An autoethnography on learning about autoethnography. *International Journal of Qualitative Methods*, **5**, Article 9. Retrieved 21 August 2008, from http://www.ualberta.ca/~iiqm/backissues/5_2/HTML/wall.htm

Wall, S. (2008) Easier said than done: Writing an autoethnography. *International Journal of Qualitative Methods*, **7**. Retrieved 21 August 2008, from http://ejournals.library.ualberta.ca/index.php/IJQM/article/view/1621

Warner, M. (1994) *Six Myths of our Time: Managing monsters.* Vintage, London.

Wollheim, R. (1984) *The Thread of Life.* Cambridge University Press, Cambridge.

6
A COMPLETE AUTOETHNOGRAPHIC ACCOUNT

CHAPTER PREVIEW

'Positions of vulnerability'
Research context and textual representation
Representation
The story
Validity
Ethics
Conclusion

The preceding chapters have mainly focused on issues to be considered in the telling of a personal story. Nested within these stories of course, are other characters that play different parts in our life events, who may have different interpretations of our story and who deserve some consideration when an account is to be published. Using the biographical details of people can be ethically challenging and this chapter will consider ways of dealing with this concern. All the usual ethical considerations of beneficence and non maleficence apply to autoethnographic research, as with any other social science research approach; however, in this case, given the lack of disguise afforded the main character, those who are related or peripheral to the story may be cast into a limelight not of their choosing.

Aimee Ebersold-Silva came into my professional sphere as a student on a masters degree for which I was responsible. I did include on the course the fascination for me of portraying the role of the individual in research, but when Aimee came to meet me to discuss my role in supervising her dissertation it was to open up a whole new perspective for us both. What follows is her attempt to juxtapose her vulnerabilities as a mental health nurse caring for drug-addicted individuals with her profound experience of being a patient earlier in her life. She not only draws attention to the issue of counter-transference in the therapeutic relationship, but draws me into her story as the supervisor of her work and illustrates the vulnerabilities of using this approach within the academy. Given the vulnerability of the clients in her story she uses a composite character to overcome the difficulty of exposing any individuals to close scrutiny. As I became drawn into the study at a personal as well as academic level I became a co-researcher whose voice can also be heard in the final work.

The composite character of Lois, a drug user, is drawn from Aimee's experience and used to interweave with her own story. My own contribution to the study demonstrates the vulnerabilities of being a supervisor of an autoethnographic dissertation in the academy.

'POSITIONS OF VULNERABILITY' (AIMEE EBERSOLD-SILVA [2004])

Resurrecting Insights

'Time, and experience influence perspective, hence events under study are in temporal transition' (Clandinin and Connelly, 2006, p. 479). These words console me as I consider resurrecting an account I completed some years ago. If every text is situated in a moment in time and place, then with every retelling of an account there is a newness of perspective and therefore development. In this spirit, I share this story with you.

During the time of writing this autoethnography, I was working as a nurse in England. I was a shared care specialist in a community drug and alcohol treatment facility. At that time, my reasons for producing this account stemmed from the internal struggle I faced balancing patient safety with patient advocacy. I questioned the degree to which 'team decisions' about a 'patient's treatment' were influenced by the medical and nursing culture of the institution. At the same time, I understood these struggles were not solely questions about team culture. They were manifestations of the complex ethical and legal issues that impact on decision making. Specifically, I was referring to decision making in regard to therapeutic limit setting with clients who were receiving drug and alcohol treatment, particularly those who had a dual addiction to both opiates and alcohol.

Through an iterative process of formulating research questions, learning about research methodology, reading the literature, and relying on personal reflection, I came to realise that another factor contributed to my struggle. This factor was my own counter-transference with patients. I realised that, in order to discern my struggle with therapeutic limit setting, I would need first to revisit the events in my life that may have impacted on the way I practised as a nurse. The implication of this raised another question for me. Why, if I was a variable in the outcome under investigation, should I exclude myself from the investigation? Shortly after I began asking these meandering questions, I learned about the method of autoethnography. I learned that autoethnography would welcome the multiple dimensions that I longed to explore. The purpose of my study finally emerged:

- to explore my experience of counter-transference in the context of my practice as a substance misuse nurse in a community drug and alcohol treatment centre

- to identify the experienced themes and meanings of my counter-transference in order to promote healing both personally and within my relationships with clients.

Presently, as I look through the lens of the past, the effect of writing this account was personally exhausting, consuming, and yet at the same time emancipating. If I could summarise an important insight that I gained, it was to be brave, and to create and share knowledge in an authentic way. From my current perspective as an educator in an undergraduate nursing programme, this insight continues to challenge me, yet drives me to persevere and fills me with feelings of liberation.

Through this chapter I hope to accomplish the following:

- to share with you the insights that brought me to choose autoethnography as a method
- to provide an example of an autoethnographic account that illustrates counter-transference and therapeutic limit setting in the context of a therapeutic nurse–patient relationship in the area of community drug and alcohol treatment
- to interweave within this account verbatim reflections of the experience of supervising an autoethnographic study. These recordings were interwoven into the original dissertation at points of parallel experience in order to highlight commonalities in vulnerability of experience
- to provide an example and discussion of a technique that can be used in autoethnography to help protect the biographical details of people portrayed in the autoethnographic account.

Exploratory Tutorial

Aimee arranged a tutorial to discuss her research proposal. This is a commonplace event, given my role as director of the masters course she is embarked on. Little did I realise that this wasn't just the meeting of a student and a teacher but the collision of two life journeys which had brought us to this point. She wanted to conduct a meaningful study, meaningful to her and the work she does. She had stumbled across autoethnography as a research method and wanted to use it. I have been writing autoethnographic accounts for some years and until this moment I had never met any one else who took it seriously. The tutorial was different from any other; I knew the risks in encouraging this approach. With the authority vested in me by the university, should I forbid it? Advise against it? Allow the student to make up her own mind? But these thoughts came afterwards; my immediate reaction was excitement, anticipation and sharing of my own resources. The tutorial ended and I felt elated, realising that if another person took this seriously it somehow validated my own experience.

RESEARCH CONTEXT AND TEXTUAL REPRESENTATION

In this autoethnography, I refer to four differing contexts, all which vary in time and place. These contexts interweave with one another to create an overall image of counter-transference. The first context was set in a post-operative ward of a large hospital in the Midwest United States. This is the setting where I narrate my experience as a post-surgical patient. The second context occurred about three years later, in a private psychotherapy practice, also in the Midwest region of the United States. In this setting, I describe my experience as a client awaiting a first psychotherapy appointment, which would soon gain me a diagnosis of post-traumatic stress disorder. The third context occurred twelve years later, at community drug and alcohol treatment centre in the East Anglia region of England. This was my place of employment while writing this narrative. The fourth and final context was set in an academic institution in England. This context offered yet another perspective to the narrative, the perspective of an academic supervisor overseeing an autoethnographic study. This experience was narrated during the time of my writing by my academic supervisor, Dr Tessa Muncey.

Committees

I sit in committees where students' research titles and research proposals are discussed and I hear talk of risk. Interestingly, not risk to Aimee from the emotional impact of her work; not risk to the clients she cares for and about; but risk to the academic world, concerns about the unworthiness of this extreme qualitative approach; concerns about research governance. Questions abound in my head, but in the controlled environment of the committee where sceptics are in the majority, I find no easy answers. How can one person's story undermine the academic world? At best, it will illuminate healthcare experiences and shed light on improving the care offered to vulnerable individuals; at worst, it will fail and no one will be aware it exists. What risk is there to the academic institution where the only risk appears to be that Aimee may fail and this is a risk she appears ready to take? My own story interweaves into Aimee's. What is proper research? What is truth? The defining experience of my life has been in conflict with the official definitions of it, and telling my story has met with all these reactions. Society fears the teenage mother as an agent of moral decline. To think how just one small, powerless, moneyless individual can bring society into a decline is laughable, but the risk that is discussed is not to the young woman or to the baby, but to the state of society. Aimee's story is attracting the same concern; not concern about her or her clients, but about the monolithic research institution.

REPRESENTATION

The narrative is layered on a number of levels. An external layer of lived experience is evident in the narratives of the many voices: a psychotherapy patient, a post-surgical patient, a patient receiving drug and alcohol treatment, an addictions nurse and an academic supervisor. A layer beneath this is also evident, as seen in the common experiences of vulnerability shared among all of the voices. A further layer beneath this exposes the internal and external complexities of personal experience weighing on each individual as they struggle to make the best decisions for themselves, or simply to survive. The use of dialogue helps to illustrate these complexities and processes. In my original dissertation, I used various fonts to help highlight this even further. Flashbacks to past experience illustrate the impact on the present, and parallel experiences highlight the commonalities of vulnerability. I give credit to texts written by Ely et al. (1991, 1997); Oleson (1992); Tierney and Lincoln (1997); Bjorklund (1998); Holmes and Gregory (1998); Tierney (2000); and Carolyn Ellis (2004). These individuals, through their writings, gave me the knowledge base and inspiration to represent the text in the way I chose. Though I have already begun, I now share with you my story.

First email

An email message arrives. I'm busy. It disappears off the end of the screen to the oblivion of the ether. I find it later and transfer it to a special folder for students' draft work. It remains unopened. I think about it every day and find a new excuse to come back to it later. I will need time to absorb it and comment. My priorities are to something else. Finally, I send it to my email address at home and in the quiet of my study I open it and read. By the juxtaposition of the two narratives I am transported to another world, the world of vulnerability of two people. I am engaged at an emotional level and very moved by the revelations. I can immediately see the impact of the stories. I reflect on the fatuous nature of the command to 'relax' when faced with a most frightening procedure, the importance of trust and all the factors that militate against it in the bureaucratic, institutional world of healthcare – the masquerading of safety for the patient when it is really the safety of the professionals and the institution that is paramount. I feel energised and send back comments with ideas for contacting another autoethnographer I had met at a conference. The wounded healer is suggested as a medium for analysis and again this collides with my first paper on qualities of the nurse wherein I conclude that nursing attracts people with a need to be needed, resonating with the myths around the wounded healer.

THE STORY

Meeting

Mary

It is my first face-to-face session with Mary. As I sit here waiting I look at everything around me. I think to myself: *I like this little room, it's a little sterile in light brown and cream, but the green plants make it feel more personal. The dimmed sound of classical music from a small radio on top of a wooden side table fills the silence and keeps me company. It allows me something to focus on if I don't want to think while I wait. I'm glad for the venetian blinds that are set in a way that I can just see the people who occasionally walk by this indoor office space. If I can barely see them, maybe they won't be able to see me.*

The main reason that I have for seeing Mary is that I have recurring nightmares and a fear of being attacked. Both while I sleep and while I'm awake I continue to run and to plan my escapes. Since my friend recommended that I get help, it has taken me about two years to decide whether I should. I look at the clock and it is almost time for my appointment. My heart begins to race and I can feel it start to pound in my chest. I think to myself, *what do I want to tell her?*

Aimee

(March, 08:45) It's Monday morning. I finally reach the car park after a twelve-mile, one-hour journey to work. The sun is bright this morning. I love walking from the car park to the treatment agency, to greet the flowers and the singing birds along my way. I see the imposing building standing tall and say to myself, 'I'm glad that I've finally made it here; I just couldn't cope working in the intensive care unit anymore.' Colleagues say I was really good with the families, and very sensitive to the patients, but that I lacked confidence with the technical aspects of the job. I think that I took the responsibility too personally. Taking things personally has been a common experience for me in most of my past nursing jobs.

In the medical psychiatric unit, the high-security mental health unit, the medical and surgical neurological unit, the specialty epilepsy unit, and the neuro-intensive care unit, I have always burned out. The job that gave me highest satisfaction was my most recent job at the needle exchange. Here, my main focus was on reducing harm. I was able to work with people as they are, many of them as outsiders to society. In a way I felt comfortable in this work, as I always felt like an outsider too. Recently I was challenged about this way of thinking, to suggest that maybe I want to be perceived in this way; to be different, to be special. Maybe I do.

I know that early this morning I have an assessment; a lady named Lois who wants help for her heroin use, and who also has a history of alcohol dependence. I enter the agency through the side door. Despite the sign that says 'FIRE EXIT ONLY' and my guilt that makes the sign grow in size everyday, I continue to enter through the side door rather than through the waiting area. I know that I avoid the waiting area for a number of reasons. One of these reasons is that I dislike secretly punching a keypad in front of people who are sitting less than arm's distance from the numbers that I press. Apart from that, I don't care for the smell of the room that seems to fluctuate in varying degrees between strong room deodoriser in the morning, to a combination of strong body odour and a stale smoke scent in the afternoon.

I make my way through the downstairs turquoise colour-schemed corridor to the main office. There I find my mailbox with a few messages left from the previous week. I never know the surprises that I will find among my messages so I have learned not to read them until I am safely at my desk. I pick up my file on Lois and read: Lois is a thirty-two-year-old single divorced lady, who wants help to stop using heroin. She has a history of problematic drug use dating back to the age of 14 and of heavy alcohol use from the age of 19. She has a four-year history of illicit opiate use and an injecting history that began two years ago.

Lois

(March, 09:45) **'Shit, I'm late!'** Lois murmurs beneath her breath as she quickly glances at her watch, jumps on her bike and throws her purse over her shoulder. She pushes down on the pedal, **'Shit that hurts,'** as she feels the denim of her blue jeans rub against the increasingly reddened hole in her groin. She thinks to herself, *I have* *waited for an appointment to be seen for about one month now, I can't be late for this, they may not see me. I am having a really difficult time finding a place to inject. My veins are solid as a rock, my groin really hurts, and even though I can still get a hit, I think it's not going to last much longer. I just can't wait to get on a prescription. I wonder what my key worker will be like? It is a pain to travel all this way so early in the morning, though if I took a bus I'd have to make two transfers. It is so unreliable and costs, although the agency gives the money back.* Lois approaches the main building and sees a number of people standing out in front of the main door. She thinks to herself, *I don't think that I know these people – hope not. I wonder if I will know anyone in the waiting area. I need to give the lady behind the window my name to let her know that I've arrived for my appointment. I don't like to say my name in front of everyone.*

Aimee: **'Lois?'** I say in a somewhat soft voice, trying not to put on an air of authority. I open the door to the waiting area and scan the room for a lady who looks at me quickly with expectancy.

Lois: **'Yes.'** She stands up abruptly, leans over to pick up her purse, and quickly glances at my hold of her file as she walks past me into the main the corridor. **'You all right?'** she says confidently as she walks a little further on through the corridor and realises that she doesn't know where she is going.

Aimee: I try to catch up to Lois and meet her side by side. **'Hello Lois, my name is Aimee.'** I hold out my hand to her in hopes that she responds to the offer of partnership through a handshake.

Lois: She turns to the side as she sees my hand come towards her and holds out her own to meet mine. Our eyes meet for a brief moment and she responds, **'Lois, nice to meet you.'**

Aimee: **'We will just go up these stairs to find a room, it's a big place here, have you been here before?'** We approach the large staircase to make our way up to the first floor corridor of rooms. This initial walk to find a room is always a little long, especially when meeting a person for the first time. I always find that if I can start a little light conversation on the way, it helps to draw attention away from the daunting numbers of rooms which surround us. As we reach the top of the staircase and turn towards the corridor I state eagerly, **'Now, I believe that there is a room available. I think it is the second to the last room on the right.'** *The room was available only five minutes earlier,* I think to myself. As we walk down the hallway, I am aware of who takes the lead. I let her go ahead.

Working

Whose Voice? You're Going Home Today!

Aimee: I look at Mary sitting across from me in a rocking chair, intently looking at me and listening deeply. I think to myself quickly, *there is so much to say, where do I start?* I decide to continue on with the story that I had started to discuss, but with a little more depth than I had intended. *I guess that there is more time to talk about other things in my life later, this feels safer.* I carry on speaking, **'So I lay in the hospital bed** following the operation that straightened my nasal septum, and removed my adenoids and wisdom teeth,' I spout out. 'Up came more blood, with the attempted melting of some ice chips in my mouth. Was this normal for the third day? Yet, I thought that I was to go home today. The nurses were very busy. I know now from being a nurse, that the mornings are truly very busy. Everything is supposed to happen in the morning. My throat still hurt from the accidental slip of the scalpel during the operation, but more than that, my breathing was becoming a little more difficult. Good, I thought to myself, the nurse has come in and I'll mention it to her.' My thoughts turned inward and I could hear the conversation taking place as if it took place just recently.

Nurse One: 'And how are you this morning?' she asks me.

Aimee: 'I'm doing alright, but my breathing is a little difficult and I'm still throwing up blood.'

Nurse One: 'You've had a lot of work done to one area and sometimes some of the blood gets into the stomach during surgery. I think that you will soon feel better. I hear that you are due to go home today, we should start to get you ready.' She rushes out of the room saying 'I'll be back soon to take out that IV.'

I sat in bed for another couple of hours, feeling still a little queasy and more and more that my breathing wasn't right. It was in fact worse I thought. I press the call button and wait.

Nurse Two: 'What would you like?' A different nurse, or maybe not, rushes in and turns off the alarm before looking at me.

Aimee: 'I feel like I am having more difficulty breathing,' I say, a little more determined and confident than the last time.

Nurse Two: 'Hmm,' she looks at me with an expression of annoyance; 'I will let your nurse know. Do you need anything else? I hear that today you get to go home!' she says in a happy, excited voice.

Aimee: 'Yeah, I guess,' I reply annoyingly. As the aid left, I again lay in the bed focusing more and more on my breathing. *Where was the nurse, I thought to myself. It has been about half an hour. I need to call her again.* I press the call button again. *I really wish someone were here with me.* I notice a wheeze to my breathing and begin to worry.

Nurse One: 'Yes,' the nurse whizzes in and looks at me quickly.

Aimee: 'I'm having more difficulty breathing,' I say now convinced.

Nurse One: 'Oh you are,' she said seriously and briskly went out of the room. As she was nearly out the door she turned her eyes quickly to mine and said, 'I'll be right back.' In she came within minutes, somebody else at her side. Quickly they spoke to each other and darted occasional looks at me. My nurse then spoke, 'We need to take you somewhere to monitor your breathing,' she said in a rushed and slightly panicked way. 'I will be right back,' and both of them rushed off out of the room.

Whose Voice? Procedures Need to be Followed

Lois and I enter into the first room on the left; I should have known that the other room would have been quickly taken. Anyway, this room is more appropriate for an assessment, it is closest to the stairway in case one of us should want to make a run for it.

> Lois: **'I'd like 60 ml of methadone, I know that this is what will hold me,'** she says confidently. She continued, **'When I received this amount a couple of years before from my GP, it really worked. I am on about the same amount of gear** [heroin] **now.'**

I think to myself quickly; I need to let her know about how her dose of methadone will be arrived at and about the assessment process. I need to establish with her the goals that she has for her treatment, make a treatment plan with her, and then set a date in pharmacy to start the process of methadone titration and stabilisation.

> Aimee: **'It sounds like you want to start methadone as soon as possible,'** I say empathetically. **'You might remember from the last time you were here that we do not give a prescription right away, that there are a number of things that we need to go through first.'**

I do empathise with Lois. She knows what has worked for her in the past, she has a nasty infection in her groin from injecting, and she is ready to start a prescription now. If she had gone to her GP, depending on who this was, she might have been able to start a prescription immediately. There is debate though about whether a quick prescription is the best way forward. When goals of treatment and boundaries of what is expected have not been set, I have seen plenty of confusion result for all involved; not only for me, but for the client, as well as the prescribing doctor.

> Lois: **'Right,'** she says. **'How long will all of this take then?'**

Whose Risk? How Long Has She Been Like This!

> Aimee: What else can help me breathe other than a ventilator? The thought jumped into my mind and stuck there. Before I realised it, through the door to the room came a trolley accompanied by two nurses, one at the side of the trolley pulling it through, and one at the back to steady it from behind. As I lifted myself onto the flat-backed trolley, a doctor appeared at my head. He lifted up one side of the trolley so that I could partially see the wall in front of me rather than the ceiling. In the end, I think that there were about 14 doctors and three nurses with me, I wonder if it had something to do with my dad being a surgeon at that hospital.
>
> Doctor One: Someone said, **'Move it, this is an emergency; get her to the OR** [Operating Room]!' I was pulled and pushed through the doorway and quickly down a corridor, into an elevator, down another corridor, and greeted by two more people. The doctor that I saw in my room stayed by my right side and talked to me. I noticed that two of the staff who accompanied him 'dropped off' and two other staff took their places. **'You were supposed to go home today!'** the doctor joked with a big smile.

My eyes focused on him as he explained to me, **'We need to help out your breathing.'** I thought to myself, I'm safe now.

Doctors Two and Three: Before I realised it, I was in a room, maybe an operating room. Suddenly my view of the wall changed into that of the ceiling. People were around me and I wasn't breathing well at all. **'Have you contacted Mike?'** one of the doctors asked. **'I can't reach him,'** said the other. My dad! I screamed to myself. I want him here but I … I don't want him to worry … but maybe he will protect me. The mood turned to tension, **'Hello Aimee, I'm doctor C. Aimee, we need to try to put something down your throat so that you can breathe easier. Can you try to relax?'** 'Oh my God,' I gag, 'I'm not able to get enough air.'

Doctor C: **'We need to try the smaller size; I don't want to do a tracky** [tracheotomy]. **OK Aimee, we are going to give you something that will try and help you relax.'** That was the last thing I remembered.

Whose Risk? Who's in Charge Here!

Lois started methadone about two weeks ago. Because of her risk of infection, I was able to get an earlier appointment for her with the doctor. Also, pharmacy staff let me do the titration of methadone as a way to speed up the process of getting Lois on to a prescription. *I hope that I haven't 'set her up for failure', as I often overhear my colleagues talk about when clients who may not be 'prepared enough' are offered a quick prescription.* The titration proceeded as I expected (last night I lay in bed anticipating the challenges I would face in the morning). As Lois said in the assessment appointment, she wanted 60 ml as a final dose. The prescription was written for 20 ml, plus 10 ml, and another 10 ml if needed. When she found out that this was written she was angry. I can still hear her voice now, **'If I receive anything less than the 60 ml I will need to use on top.'** I said that I would discuss with the doctor again about what she felt that she needed in order to abstain from illicit heroin.

My extremist viewpoint took hold. *It would go either of two ways, I thought. Either we would prescribe what she wants with a number of contingencies, i.e. attendance of appointments and a plan for reduction if she uses any illicit drugs on top; or she will stay on this dose, test positive on drug screens, and be discharged from treatment. I'm sure that colleagues would remind me in this situation that 'it is the client who has to make the decision to change'.* During the titration I watched for signs of withdrawal. I even followed the opiate withdrawal checklist to let her know that I wanted to be as objective as possible.

However, I also trusted Lois in how she felt. Knowing that ultimately she wanted a higher dose of methadone, I provided the additional doses of methadone as a titration based on her subjective reports, even though the objective signs were not as telling. Was I colluding with her or was I valuing and trusting her experience? I came to the conclusion that I provided the methadone according to the prescription and followed titration guidelines. There was minimal risk to me, but how has this process affected our relationship? As Lois said, **'it is clear who has the power here.'**

Whose Vulnerability? Where is my Notepad?

Doctor C: 'Aimee?' I wake to someone touching my arm. 'Aimee, you are not able to speak. You have a tube in and so you can't talk. Can you hear me?' A fuzzy person comes into focus, I recognise him and I nod. 'We need to keep the tube in until the swelling goes down,' he explains. *All I can think of is that I want to go to my room; I know that I will feel safer in my room.*

Dad: What seemed like hours later, I looked over to my dad who was sitting alongside my bed. 'The tube is pretty small,' he said to me. 'They needed to use a paediatric size because you had too much swelling.' I look at him and then look past him into the room. 'Your mom has gone out to the hallway because she is having a hard time seeing you like this.' *I think to myself how good it is that both of them are here. I feel safe knowing that they are close by. My sister! Is she here? I really don't want her to see me like this; I don't want her to know I am like this. Our emotions often merge.*

Nurse Three: We are interrupted by my sudden gag and the stark sound of an alarm. I sputter and cough, and cough again. I can't breathe. A nurse rushes in, 'I think that you need suction.' She quickly tears open a plastic packet, pulls out a long thin plastic tube and shoves it inside the tube in my mouth. *I can't catch my breath.* 'This will make you cough,' she says. A huge cough comes and I gasp and cough again, and gasp. 'Relax,' I hear her say abruptly.

Nurse Four: Night falls quickly; I look forward to the wall and notice the television. 'It is New Year's Eve,' a nurse says to me gently as she walks around the bed and looks at the various kinds of equipment stuck to me. I am thankful because at this point I have a suction device in my hand so that I can clear the back of my throat when I need to. This hopefully reduces the need for me to have the nurse do it.

'I need to take some blood from your wrist, is that ok with you?' the nurse asks softly. 'This will hurt a little.' A sharp stabbing pain shoots up my wrist as the needle penetrates my skin. 'There, I'm all finished. While I am here and you are awake, I'd like to reposition you.'

Aimee: *Oh no, the repositioning, I think to myself. How will this nurse be? Gentle with the turns or like the other, flipping me over like a sack of potatoes. Once I move, I will start to cough, I won't be able to breathe, the alarm will go off, and then I'll need to be suctioned. I still won't be able to breathe, and the alarm will continue to go off. Then again, I'm awake and I may as well do it now.* I fumble quickly for my trusty wad of paper and a pencil, I write as legibly as I am able. The lights are off and I am laid in a somewhat flat position strapped to tubes. I try to find an empty space on the paper among notes to my boyfriend, my mom, and dad. I write to the nurse, 'I might need to cough, but my throat hurts.'

Whose Vulnerability? Where is the Breathalyser?

Colleague: **'Hey Aimee,'** a colleague yells over to me in the corridor. **'Come over here,'** as she makes a motion for me to come closer. We look over at Lois who is waiting in the corner of the room, her arms folded across her chest. **'I think that Lois has started a little on the drink. Do you want us to start breathalysing her before she picks up?'**

Aimee: *Oh shit, I think to myself. What should I do? Did I miss something that was obvious to other people?* **'What do you typically do in this situation?'** I ask, afraid of what I might hear.

Colleague: **'Sometimes a breathalyser test will let you know if the person is developing a problem with the drink. It puts a limit on their drinking.'**

Aimee: **'Ok, I think that you're right. Go ahead if you don't mind doing it.'**

I should have anticipated how this would have worked out. Lois was positive for alcohol and she was angry for being tested without me telling her about it first. I didn't at all think about the consequences if she breathalysed positive. I care so much about what my colleagues think of me! Why could I not step back from this situation and say to my colleague that I first wanted to discuss the breathalyser intervention with Lois before I started to apply it. Instead, I responded by saying to myself that I needed to act now, and if I didn't, I'd appear like an unsafe practitioner. Why didn't I just ask her if she had been drinking and then have a brief discussion with her about it? Lois is rightly upset.

Aimee: **'Lois, I think that we need to talk about what happened the other day in the pharmacy,'** I say in an apologetic tone. **'I apologise for having the pharmacy staff breathalyse you without me first talking to you about it. Do you know the reasons why we use the breathalyser?'**

Lois: **'I haven't a clue. I came here because I wanted help for heroin and now what I'm told is that I "won't get" if I breathalyse positive. If it's a Friday, I can't collect for that day or for my weekend doses. How is this supposed to help me?'** she says annoyingly.

Aimee: I explain to Lois that first and foremost, the combination of alcohol and methadone can lead to overdose and that we are responsible for safety in the prescription that we give out. In addition, I say, **'I know that you have had a problem with alcohol in the past. Breathalysing you daily before you pick up methadone might give you that extra incentive not to over-use alcohol and might help prevent you from going back to heavy drinking.'**

Lois: **'So I will just wait to drink until after I pick up methadone. I just don't get it. If I test positive two days in a row you will stop my prescription,'** she says, completely ignoring my monologue of the importance of breathalysing. **'I've become dependent on my prescription. My life is getting sorted out. Do you want to me go back to injecting into my groin?'**

Aimee: *I could take this further,* I think to myself. *I could speak with her about breathalysing her before our sessions, which is also part of the policy for safety here.* I decide that today I'd better not discuss any more limits. We end the session together and I walk to my desk feeling mentally bruised. I pull out my blue rolling office chair, sit down, and hold the sides of my face in my hands.

As I exhale, thoughts come marching into my consciousness. *What kind of a nurse am I? Am I insensitive to what Lois needs? If she were still prescribed by her GP and picking up in a pharmacy outside of this place, the breathalyser would probably not be part of her treatment at all. Are we right in putting a limit on Lois's drinking to help prevent one type of dependence if it interferes with her receiving help for the dependence she sought help for?* I suppose that I am more aware of these dilemmas because one of my roles is working with GPs to promote the shared care of substance misuse treatment. My thoughts stream on … *It seems to all come down to philosophies of treatment* and on … *I am not very popular with some GPs who think that I represent an archaic way of working and I'm not very popular with the treatment agency who think that I am unable to manage how some GPs prescribe.*

Thoughts about the past seep in. *I recall memories of nurses who took care of me in the past. I recall how it felt to be dependent on the kind of care that they gave, including whether or not I was listened to.* **'Risk,'** I say out loud, as if to purge the thought from my consciousness. *Risk and interventions, this is where it all gets complicated.* I think of a scenario that I experienced when I worked in the needle exchange. A client said to me, **'I will share other people's needles if you do not give me long blue and greens** [needles] **to inject into my groin. You know that I'm Hep** [hepatitis] **C positive. Besides, I'm being treated for my blood clot.'** *Whose risk should I consider in this intervention, my professional risk or the physical risk to this person and possibly others?*

Ending

I just Passed over All Control and Had Faith

Aimee: 'The nurse and I finished the full schedule of events as I imagined it would transpire. However, this nurse worked more gently than the other. She was more relaxed in her voice, worked around me at a slower pace, explained things to me, and gave me a little more control in how we did things. *Control,* I think to myself. *I focus on my breath, trying to match it to the sounds of my machine. Sometimes I lose track of the rhythm and it all goes out of sync and then the alarms start. I always feel in varying degrees like I am choking. I just keep breathing through the tenacious mass that lines my only airway, a tube. The only way I can cope with this is to let go, to focus, relax, and breathe through the feeling of choking. I have no control. I have only faith in a God who I do not understand and faith in people to help. What a test. For the first time, I am not embarrassed about my dad's silly inventions; this time it is a flashlight by my side to wake him at night if I need.* 'I just realise that I am talking about the same story that I chose to talk about when I first met you. It's interesting how what I focus on in the story changes as time goes on.' Mary and I sit together in her room in the same place as always, her in the rocking chair and me on the sofa. Today is our last session in what has already been about six years. 'The work here has been difficult. It is difficult because it is hard to grasp hold of; it is abstract and elusive.'

> Mary: 'When we first met, I could barely hear you speak. You have shared with me a great deal throughout these years.'
> Aimee: 'I recall that when we first met, every time that I spoke I would cry. Just the sound of my voice would be enough to start it all off. Thank you for your patience

with me.' *She was always there for me, her voice so consistent in response that I could predict what she would say when I presented troubles. In time, I acquired her voice to give me strength. Now I am on my way to developing my own voice, a voice without tears.* 'I know that I have more changes to make, but I feel more able to cope now.'

If you want help, we are here to help

I decided not to breathalyse Lois before our sessions. I needed to show some trust in what she told me about her drinking. I wanted to give some of the control back to her. In a session we had together, Lois and I had the following conversation.

Lois: 'I think that I'm dependent on alcohol. I keep failing the breathalyser test more and more. I'm missing doses of methadone all of the time now and I'm basically buying it off the street. I want an alcohol detox, but I don't think that I'd be able to stay off of the alcohol. I keep attending these appointments, but I'm not sure why I'm still here.'

Aimee: 'The alcohol has affected what you have been able to receive from this place. You eventually received 60 ml of methadone from the doctor, which is what you thought would help. Now, this has now been reduced to 40 ml due to your drinking *(I wonder if she's buying 60 ml of methadone off the streets?)* On the other hand, you have done really well in other areas. You continue to attend appointments with me and you continue to avoid heroin. The most recent drug screen proves your effort.'

Lois: 'I'm glad for those drug screens. They are the only thing that I have going for me,' she says eyes downcast. 'At first I didn't want to admit it about my alcohol use, but you were right. I never completed any of the drink diaries that you gave me to do, and when I told you about my drinking I didn't tell you all of it. In fact, I keep telling you that I want to detox, but I'm not sure if I really do.'

Aimee: 'If you want the help Lois, we are here to help.' *I wonder though, do we?*

I didn't know it, but this was the last session that I would have with Lois. She stopped attending further appointments and never made contact. In hindsight, maybe I did set her up to fail, or at least I prolonged the process. I trusted that Lois wanted to make a change with her alcohol use. I trusted the reasons that she gave me for not completing her homework. I even provided her with a pen and paper. I trusted what she told me about her drinking even though she never completed a drink diary. Had I done a breathalyser test in our sessions, would I have learned that she was consuming more than she told me? Maybe Lois lost trust in me, that I was unable to provide enough limits to her behaviour. I just wanted to give her a little more freedom to breathe, to do things in her own time.

After talking with the team about Lois, they all thought that I needed to discharge her from treatment. I guess that I agree; *I can't hold a slot for someone who is not making contact. There are so many more people who are waiting to be seen. I will need to write a letter to her, but I really dislike this way of ending a relationship.* I pencil down the 'get in touch letter' in my small notebook, and hand it in for typing.

Dear Lois,

I'm sorry that you have been unable to attend the last couple of appointments with me. Would you make contact with me within the next two weeks to let me know if you wish for further contact? If I do not hear from you by this time, I will assume that you are no longer interested in further contact with me and will discharge you from the service. You would be welcome to re-refer yourself at any time should you wish.

All the best,

Aimee

'There, I'll put it in the post this evening. I can't believe how quick I've become in writing these kinds of letters.' *I still am very concerned about how I come across in a letter. Words can be so loaded with all sorts of assumptions.* 'I've got so much more to do now before I go home.' *Maybe I should just finish up and be done for the day. Then again, I'd need to go down to the office and answer phones. I'm a disaster with transferring calls. Maybe I will just take time owing and take care of myself. I wonder though what others will think (this damn theme again). I would hate to be seen as a slacker. Then again, I think I am seen as someone who has a hard time letting go. Both of these traits are equally nothing to boast about in this place of work.*

The Story Continues

When I began to tell you about the making of this story, I spoke broadly about how I came to decide on this type of study, and how I chose to represent my experience. I then shared with you my story, to provide an example of how my experience, and representation of it, offered insight from multiple perspectives. In my original dissertation, I provided evidence from the literature to give justification for the importance of studying the experience of counter-transference not only in practitioners, but in 'wounded nurses' in particular. Also through the literature, I provided justification for why the method of autoethnography provides a unique means of highlighting the complexities involved in this experience.

However, when it comes to using an individual story's story to research a particular subject, this will quite often be met with questions concerning validity and ethics. For many, even with rational argument, the use of autoethnography as a research method will be seen as nothing more than 'sheer self-indulgence'. In my original dissertation, I discuss in detail the methods I used to portray my experience as a patient and practitioner, as well as with the clients I worked with. I also fully discuss my study in relation to validity and ethical standards. For the purposes of this context, I would like to narrow my focus and reflect only on Lois; her validity, and the ethics of using a composite character.

Second Tutorial

Since starting to supervise Aimee. I am emboldened to include autoethnography as a research technique in my social sciences module. Intended as a discussion about the contribution to research of the individual story, I expected stimulated discussion. I received some angry, negative, anonymous evaluations, the most stinging of which was that this was sheer 'self indulgence.' I have been called a liar, self-indulgent and unethical before and suddenly I fear for Aimee. I believe that I can only be responsible for what I say, not how it is received, but the unenlightened responses hurt. I want to retaliate but resist with wise counsel. The echoes of previous questions haunt me.

VALIDITY

In reflecting on the validity of Lois to represent my experience of working with individuals engaged in substance abuse treatment, I will first provide details of how I developed her character and her experience of treatment. By definition, Lois was a composite character, as she was a representation of many clients with whom I worked during my time as a nurse in addictions treatment. The methods I used to create Lois were based on my field notes, and from a case study I wrote of my experience working with a client. I compiled the field notes over a three-week period, and included my experiences both in the treatment agency and in a primary care practice. I wrote field notes daily, retrospectively following each day of work. They included every aspect of my working day; my work with clients, conversations with colleagues, emotions, and reflections about the events. I used alternative names when making field notes about clients or colleagues. I also reviewed letters that I wrote to clients. In highlighting my past nursing experience in relation to working with patients, I reflected on autobiographical journal writings of my past clinical nursing experiences.

So what do these procedures mean for judging the validity of a composite character in autoethnographic research? To answer this question, I refer back to the ontological and epistemological paradigm of my original study, constructivism. From this viewpoint, underlying the study was my belief that the nature of reality can be individually constructed, not only discovered (Henwood, 1996; Lincoln and Guba, 2000). It held the assumption that there are multiple social realities (Hammersley, 1992), and that subjective and created knowledge can be counted as true and valid. According to these assumptions, my subjective process of writing field notes, interpreting them, and representing them in the text represented my reality. The question then becomes, does the representation of my reality appear valid to you? Carloyn Ellis has suggested that autoethnography be judged as valid through the concept of 'verisimilitude' (Ellis, 2004). This idea suggests that validity is determined by whether the text evokes in you a feeling that what I describe is 'lifelike, believable and possible'.

Why does knowing the subject of the research make people feel so vulnerable? There are real people in randomised controlled trials, but they are disguised and hidden; this is paraded as objective and morally superior. People who condemn autoethnography appear to take the moral high ground and yet my etymological dictionary tells me that research is just 'intensive searching' or 'investigation directed towards discovery'. It is the powerful institution of research that changes this into defining a proper way to do research and by definition an improper one. Aimee is experiencing these same reflections on her work. She needs to protect herself. Seeing this vulnerability makes me more determined to support the process, to value it. My own journey has been enhanced by this study. I believe that emotional impact should become a legitimate research evaluation and that distance from the individual is a safety device for the researcher.

ETHICS

In reflecting on the ethics of using a composite character, there are two arguments that I wish to raise. Both relate to power relations, the first being more global, and the second more personal. The first point I wish to highlight stems from traditional ethnographic accounts, though it can apply to any research where a particular group is portrayed without sufficient background about the perspective of the researcher. In the past, traditional ethnographic accounts were typically criticised for how researchers represented the 'subjects' of their research without providing information about their own perspectives. The concern was that, without having an understanding of the researcher perspective, a person reading the research would not be fully informed about how researcher influences may affect what is portrayed about the group. Embedded in this were implications of the power relationships between the researcher and the cultural group that was under study. These criticisms of 'representation and legitimation' (Brewer, 2000) were one of the influencing factors leading to the inclusion of the researcher's perspective, and hence to autoethnographic methods. From this perspective, I argue that autoethnography addresses the power imbalances that can arise from more traditional forms of research.

Work in Progress

Aimee and I sit side by side in a 'work in progress' seminar. The student presenting her work has taken existing statistical data and is re-examining it from another perspective. There are no new ideas, no imagination; it is safe, and has the 'so what' factor for me. The sophistication of the statistical language drowns out audience participation except to clarify some underlying assumptions. The results mirror those of a thousand quantitative studies, namely: that disease, and educational and class status impact on health status in old age. This study is safe and predictable, but tells nothing of the human experience behind the numbers. Aimee leans into me and whispers 'just imagine: this will pass where mine might not.' She's referring to the safety of doing anodyne research.

In relation to power imbalances and how this addresses the ethical decision of whether to use a composite character, I address the theme of power imbalances again, but from a more personal perspective. As I believe decisions for all research are context-specific, I will speak about the specific benefits and drawbacks of using a composite character for this study. One of the greatest benefits I found in using a composite character is that it protected the individual identities of those under study. In the context of my study, I was a nurse within the treatment team, the individuals I worked with were engaged in treatment, and the study group was small enough for individual identification. The benefits of being an insider to the institution provided a credible perspective, yet one that proved to be a challenge. The power imbalances were large, even with me stating my perspective. Utilising a composite character allowed me to portray the complex and personally challenging experience of providing care to those individuals with dual addictions to alcohol and opiates. It also allowed me to give a voice to the clients who I worked with, albeit my voice, without jeopardising their treatment experience.

This leads, however, to the drawbacks of using a composite character. Again, with regard to power imbalance, does the use of a composite character really give a voice to individuals? One could argue that a composite character actually reduces an individual experience by providing to the reader only a single representation. In addition, haven't I advocated for the emancipating experience of telling one's story? Lastly, wouldn't the telling of each individual's story hold more power to an outside authority than providing only my own interpretation?

These are very challenging and important questions. The rationale I give for my decision to use a composite character lies again in the context of this study. In reflecting on possible research questions, methodologies, and the impact of these on personal relationships at all levels in the institution, I decided that I should study my own counter-transference. I decided to discern whether the interventions I provided as a nurse were based on issues pertaining to my past experiences. I decided to unravel my assumptions that the breathalyser intervention was an example of a paternalistic intervention driven more by team culture than by evidence. In the end, I looked to a relational ethic of care (Pauly and James, 2005) to preserve both my collegial relationships and support harmony within the institution. In conclusion, my decision of whether to use a composite character was grounded in the particular context of my research question. This included the setting of my research, my relationships to those impacted by the study, and my main purpose for pursuing this particular study.

CONCLUSION

In closing, I leave you with a final reflection from my dissertation, written by Dr Tessa Muncey.

I read a quote by WB Yeats this morning: 'Education is not the filling of a pail, but the lighting of a fire.' Shouldn't some research do the same, fire up the emotions? After all, we exist on more than the thinking/physical level. Aimee's metaphorical story of water makes me think of the impact of water on fire, stories will drown and people will be reduced to molecules just as pebbles are to sand. In her book Opening to Spirit: Contacting the Healing Power of the Chakras, *Caroline Arewa (1998) describes spiritual and psychological correspondences of the sacral chakra. I am not surprised that these are water, low self worth when disturbed, and fear of emotion. This fits the metaphorical story so well and reinforces the importance of autoethnography, for me, in helping to develop a sense of self vital to the wounded healer. While Aimee's research speaks volumes about the human spirit, I again reflect on people's fears of identifying with research participants. I reflect that if I were telling my 'wise woman' about this research, I would feel so proud to be associated with it. When I think of defending it against sceptical colleagues, my shroud of vulnerability descends again.*

Summary

- Portraying other characters in your story can be ethically challenging. Including them as composite characters or co-researchers, or writing co-constructed stories can overcome the difficulties.
- Autoethnography addresses the power imbalances that can arise from more traditional forms of research.
- Relational ethics are important to preserve clients or family members' confidentiality; to maintain harmony within an institution, whether that be work, family or education; and to conserve collegial and personal relationships.
- Every retelling of a story can bring a new perspective and allows knowledge to be shared in an authentic way.
- Multiple voices can be distinguished in a text by changing the colour or nature of the font.

REFERENCES

Arewa, C.S. (1998) *Opening to Spirit: Contacting the healing power of the chakras and honouring African spirituality.* Thorsons, London.

Bjorklund, D. (1998) *Interpreting the Self: Two hundred years of American autobiography.* University of Chicago Press, Chicago, IL.

Brewer, J. (2000) *Ethnography.* Open University Press, Buckingham.

Clandinin, D.J. and Connelly, F. (2006) Narrative Inquiry. In J.L. Green, G. Camilli and P.B. Elmore (Eds) *Handboook of Complementary Methods in Educational Research.* Lawrence Erlbaum Associates, Mahwah, NJ.

Ebersold-Silva, A. (2004) 'Positions of vulnerability: An autoethnographic study'. Masters dissertation, University of Cambridge, Cambridge.

Ellis, C. (2004) *The Ethnographic I: A methodological novel about autoethnography. (Ethnographic Alternatives).* Alta Mira Press, Oxford.

Ely, M., Vinz, R., Downing, M. and Anzul, M. (1997) *On Writing Qualitative Research: Living by words.* Falmer Press, London.

Ely, M., Anzul, M., Friedman, T., Garner, D. and McCormack-Steinmetz, A. (1991) *Doing Qualitative Research: Circles within circles.* Falmer Press, London.

Hammersley, M. (1992) *What's Wrong with Ethnography? Methodological explorations.* Routledge, London.

Henwood, N. (1996) Qualitative Inquiry: Perspectives, Methods and Psychology. In J. Richardson (Ed.) *Handbook of Qualitative Research Methods for Psychology and The Social Sciences.* BPS Books, London, ch. 3.

Holmes, V. and Gregory, D. (1998) Writing poetry: A way of knowing nursing. *Journal of Advanced Nursing,* **28**(6), 1191–4.

Lincoln, Y.S. and Guba, E.G. (2000) Paradigmatic Controversies, Contradictions and Emerging Confluences. In N.K. Denzin and Y.S. Lincoln (Eds) *Handbook of Qualitative Research.* Sage, London, ch. 6.

Oleson, V. (1992) Extraordinary Events and Mundane Ailments: The contextual dialectics of the embodied self. In C. Ellis and M.G. Flaherty (Eds) *Investigating Subjectivity: Research on lived experience.* Sage, London, ch. 10.

Pauly, B. and James, S. (2005) Living Relational Ethics in Healthcare. In D. Freshwater and C. Johns (Eds) *Transforming Nursing through Reflective Practice.* Blackwell Publishing, Oxford.

Tierney, W. (2000) Undaunted Courage: Life history and the postmodern challenge. In N.K. Denzin and Y.S. Lincoln (Eds) *Handbook of Qualitative Research.* Sage, London, ch. 20.

Tierney, W. and Lincoln, Y.S. (1997) *Representation and the Text: Reframing the narrative voice.* State University of New York Press, Albany, NY.

7
THE AUTOETHNOGRAPHIC PROCESS: Starting a New Story

CHAPTER PREVIEW

Songwriting and autoethnography (David Carless)
Writing and not writing
All I have is questions
West village, New York city
Finding – or creating – hope
Reflections on connections
Letting go

I can't let this book be finished before I mention some of the exquisite synchronicities that have guided its development – from the papers that appear just at the right time to the people who materialise just when I need them. Meeting David Carless was one such event. Stumbling across him at the Congress of Qualitative Inquiry in Urbana-Champaign, in a workshop run by Tami Spry about performance autoethnography, seemed to bode well for establishing a shared interest. Listening to his and Kitrina Douglas's interpretation of their research in song in a creative methods workshop brought home to me the real meaning of resonance (Douglas and Carless, 2005). At the point that I was realising that I needed a new voice to try to summarise the whole process of autoethnography, I found myself in a coffee shop in Leeds talking to David about the book. With only the shortest brief of what I wanted the chapter to include, he has captured the essence of what it is to portray a new experience in a creative, refreshing way.

I am only sorry that I can't bring his music alive in this written text. However, his fascinating perspective on writing songs both for personal and professional reasons summarises beautifully the contribution that autoethnography can make to the research world, and echoes many of the issues that have arisen throughout this text, not least of which is the way that the ideas come from beyond that thinking part of the brain; to release them it is necessary to let go of a conscious desire to shape what comes.

SONGWRITING AND AUTOETHNOGRAPHY
(DAVID CARLESS)

I have been writing songs since I was nineteen, long before I wrote my first research paper. Looking back, songwriting has been a way by which I have explored my experiences and my place in the world. Songwriting has brought me understandings and insights and, perhaps, allowed me to create personal stories which map my life and more closely fit my experience. In Lewis's (2006) terms, it has given me 'stories to live by'. Performing those songs for others may be seen as a public representation of self through which I seek *connection* through identification, understanding, shared experience, common ground.

- I see songwriting as a form of autoethnography which involves 'setting a scene, telling a story, weaving intricate connections among life and art, experience and theory, evocation and explanation ... and then letting go, hoping for readers who will bring the same careful attention to your words in the context of their own lives' (Holman Jones, 2005, p. 765).
- I see songwriting as a form of lyric inquiry which 'draws upon non-rationalist and non-discursive ways of knowing in order to engage in inquiry practices and produce written forms that have, up to now, been undervalued or ignored in scholarly discourses ... Such research foregrounds the personal and the aesthetic' (Neilsen, 2008, p. 94).
- I see songwriting as a form of narrative inquiry where 'narrative is retrospective meaning making – the shaping or ordering of past experience. Narrative is a way of understanding one's own and others' actions, of organising events and objects into a meaningful whole, and of connecting and seeing the consequences of actions over time' (Chase, 2005, p. 656).
- I see songwriting as a form of arts-based or arts-informed research in which '*the creative inquiry process* of arts-informed research is defined by an openness to the expansive possibilities of the human imagination ... we infer that researchers can learn from artists about matters of process. That is, the processes of art making inform the inquiry in ways congruent with the artistic sensitivities and technical (artistic) strengths of the researcher in concert with the overall spirit and purpose of the inquiry' (Cole and Knowles, 2008, p. 61).
- I see songwriting as located at a blurred intersection between autoethnography, lyric inquiry, narrative inquiry and arts-based/arts-informed research.

From a position on this blurred intersection, I want in this chapter to focus explicitly on the *processes* of songwriting in the faith that, as Cole and Knowles (2008) suggest, (autoethnographic) researchers might be able to learn something about matters of process from (songwriting) artists. To do so, I offer an autoethnographic account in which I attempt to follow Holman Jones's (2005) advice to set a scene, tell a story, weave connections among life and art, experience and theory, evocation and explanation … and then let go.

WRITING AND NOT WRITING

Songwriting feels to me to be both the most 'difficult' and the 'easiest' form of writing I engage with and explore. When I am *not* writing, it isn't so much difficult as *impossible*. Between songs, I feel like I will never be able to write another song and every song feels like it will be the last. I wonder where inspiration might come from. Even though I might be aware of a whole world of stories around me, I feel like I have nothing to say, that there is nothing *there* to write. Sometimes, it feels like I have no music *in* me. I may not play the guitar for days on end, I may not write a song for months on end. When I do pick up a guitar, the music that comes seems to hold little in the way of new things, it leads nowhere. Occasionally, I've tried to *force* a song to come – by *making* myself sit with a guitar, play and sing. But whatever comes never seems to *work* as a song; as Suzanne Vega has put it, 'it doesn't even sing' (cited in Zollo, 2003, p. 571). Put simply, nothing really comes – no music that *sings,* no words that *speak*. At times like these, it seems I simply cannot write.

And then one day, seemingly out of the blue, I have some time with my guitar and a new song starts to happen. I never see a song coming and when one starts to come I can never quite believe it. At these times, I am not *trying* to write a song because there is no need to try. I am not aware of applying effort, of working, of deliberately moving in any particular direction. Instead, it very often feels like the song is *happening*, being created, without my conscious effort. Some sections happen fast, as much time as they take to sing; other sections resist happening and I have to put the guitar down, walk around the room or take a break. After an hour, two hours, or perhaps a morning, the song is finished. Writing it and singing it those first few times brings me alive, excites me, energises me. It is only afterwards that a sense of tiredness comes.

So, on a songwriting day – when I am actually writing – I cannot say that songwriting is 'difficult'. On a difficult–easy continuum, 'easy' would be closer to the truth. But on any other day, to describe the process as 'easy' would be a lie because songwriting, at these times, is *way* beyond difficult. As I say, it seems impossible. But what is the difference between a writing and a not-writing day? What distinguishes these days from each other? What is it that allows writing to happen? What has to be in place for creativity to occur? It is these questions that I would like to begin to consider here. To this end, I offer a story in three parts which I hope *shows* – in an evocative and embodied way – my experiences around writing one particular song called 'Stay Close'. Through a combination of the story and reflection on the story, I want to suggest some links between the creative processes involved in songwriting and the creative processes that are perhaps required to write good autoethnography.

ALL I HAVE IS QUESTIONS

I drove us through the city, the dark and endlessly wet streets. We had loaded his belongings – bags, boxes and clothes – into the back of my van ten minutes earlier, before he had pushed the key back through the letterbox of his small rental house after closing the door for the last time. Bradley, my partner, was moving in with me.

I was happy that Bradley would never have to return to the dingy little rental house in the city centre. I felt excited to be about to share a home with him. But as we drove my excitement waned, to be replaced by fear and doubt, as he told me that he had decided to leave the UK and move back to New York in five months time. I already knew that his base was New York and that his work required travel and now, once more, relocation.

After just a few weeks of living together I also knew – with him – that his work was not working. I began to see its consequences written on his face and body when he came home in the evening. Despite wanting him to stay, despite wanting us to continue living together, despite the fear that our relationship would be over if he moved across the Atlantic, despite the prospect of living alone again, I resigned myself to him leaving. It seemed like it was the right thing for him to do and I could see no alternative. I began a five-month build up to what I envisaged as an agonising parting at Heathrow airport. All I could see was endings.

I had started talking to a few friends about Bradley's decision to leave the country and how I was feeling about it. I had long talks on the phone with my friend Kitrina who through our conversations offered understanding, wisdom and support. I met for coffee with Julie who made me cake, listened to my story, empathised and gave me a hug. After telling him about my time with Bradley and his impending return to New York, I received a caring and encouraging email from Brett:

> For what its worth, and I don't mean to sound patronizing etc, enjoy it mate. Easier said than done I know. Moving back to NY will be shit. But, it might not happen. If it does, I'm sure there is a university there that would love you. So it could be good!!! What I'm trying to say in a rather clumsy way I suppose is enjoy life mate. You deserve it, and whatever the future, you'll deal with it – you're a great guy, and sometimes things go well for the good guy too!

Around the same time I received an email back from my friend Deb in Australia who wrote:

> How fabulous that you are in love. Don't worry too much just yet about the fact that Bradley might be heading home in summer. When I met Steve he had about four months left on his visa. Sometimes things work out simply because they have to. You just have to stay open to the possibilities.

Bradley, too, seemed to be positive and confident about our future together, telling me of ideas he had about how we could continue to spend time together in the US and in Europe and ways that we might be able to share a home again in the future.

These different responses had helped me and comforted me over the previous days, a time when my thoughts were a good deal less positive. Perhaps these others' words were in my head, perhaps they were in my heart, as I spent a quiet weekend on my own while Bradley went to Italy on a work trip. It was our first weekend apart since he'd moved in and I was already missing him being around. I was trying hard to avoid thinking about how our separation would feel when he left for New York. I had no answers to the question of what would happen to us – or me – when he moved. Would he return? Would I move with him? How could I make a life in a country in which I had no citizenship rights; a country in which a male–male partnership counted for nothing with the immigration authorities? All I had were questions. All I had were fears.

WEST VILLAGE, NEW YORK CITY

In our kitchen on Sunday morning I picked up the guitar I'd bought just ten days previously. Already this instrument felt familiar and, somehow, it was comforting just sitting with it. This guitar already felt like a friend. Part of the familiarity might have been down to this new instrument being the exact same shape (and make) as my first 'serious' guitar which I'd bought 17 years previously. Through playing this first guitar for ten years or more, 'we' had grown to fit each other, and the manufacturer's trade-mark shape and feel had become familiar to me. Another part of the familiarity, though, might have been down to the experiences of the previous two weeks.

I'd bought the guitar from a music shop in the West Village on my first visit to New York with Bradley. It was the first instrument I'd picked up in that store and, although I tried many others, this one seemed to fit me right from the start. I sat in the partitioned acoustic room trying it out on various songs. I wanted to sing too but felt inhibited in the store. I found myself quietly singing a line here or there when I had the room to myself. And this guitar was working! Songs were there and bubbling out as I played and, even though I resisted giving them voice, they would still break through. Other customers milled around looking at guitars while I played, occasion-ally casting me – or the guitar – a glance. One or two made a brief comment,

'Sounds good, man.'

'Thanks, yeah, I like this one.'

At one point I had a nice rhythm going on a new piece I'd written a few weeks ear-lier, when one of the other customers began tapping out a percussion part using the coins in his pockets to approximate a basic drum kit. I guess he started playing quietly, I don't remember a beginning – the percussion just suddenly seemed to *be there*. And it worked, it fitted perfectly. Typical! I thought. I'd never managed to find a drummer or percussionist who was able to find rhythms that worked with my music and here, in a music shop in New York, some random guy was tapping out a perfect part on his pocket change while he browsed the guitars!

'That's great, that really works. You must be a drummer!' I said. He laughed.

'Yeah, we sounded good! Nice song. I am, well, I was. I was a session player for a long time.'

'Do you fancy getting a band together?' I asked, half meaning it. 'We'll have to be quick – I'm only in town for a week!' He laughed again.

'Thanks for the compliment. But no, I only really work on my own stuff now.'

I left the store after almost three hours of playing and chatting about guitars. I returned the next day and played the same guitar some more. After a couple more hours I left again to meet Bradley for coffee. On my way I checked my emails to find a two-day-old message from my mum telling me that her mother had died. Mum didn't have a number to call me and had decided to hold off telling me the news until my grandmother's funeral arrangements had been made. The funeral was to be the day after I returned from the US and mum asked if I would be willing to perform a song – one of my own called 'One Step at a Time' – at the funeral service. It was that request that made me begin to cry, quietly and unnoticed, amid the laptops and the crowds in the Apple store on Fifth Avenue.

It was also that request that made my mind up about buying the guitar. My grandmother's death reminded me that time is short, that I must make the most use of whatever time I have. From this place, I justified the cost of the guitar as an irrelevance, as insignificant. It would be money well spent if even one new song appeared as a consequence. There was also the practical problem that I would need a guitar to play the song at her funeral. My guitar was in Leeds; I was flying into London; and her funeral would be in Devon the day after I returned. I *could* borrow a guitar but I knew any old guitar wouldn't do – it wouldn't do for this particular song, which demanded certain qualities of an instrument, and it wouldn't do for my grandmother's funeral.

The next day, I returned to the music shop and bought the guitar. The first time 'we' performed in public together was at my grandmother's funeral four days later. I leant on that instrument for support in the little chapel that afternoon. I held it to me closely, feeling its body resonate against mine, trusting its notes to ring clear and true, as I stood beside my grandmother's wicker coffin and faced the assembled group of family and friends. The guitar's presence – its feel – comforted me. With this guitar I was not alone, at a time when I needed help to *do* this song, to not mess up, to pay tribute to my granny. The guitar delivered. We were in relationship: me and it.

FINDING – OR CREATING – HOPE

On my own in our kitchen that Sunday morning, I tuned the guitar down to 'open-D' and strummed all six strings, low to high, with my thumb. The sound filled the room, bouncing back at me off the tiled floor and stone walls. In this tuning, the six strings are tuned in such a way that together, without requiring any strings to be fretted with the left hand, they ring to create a D major chord. I leant in to the guitar harder, strumming the full chord with a pick now. I let the new phosphor-bronze strings ring uninterrupted. From just one weighty strum, the six strings resonated through the back of the guitar and I could feel the movement of the wood against my stomach as I sat at the kitchen table. The low D string supplied a powerful bass drone below the higher notes – F#, an A, another D – which shimmered and sang on and on, crisp and clear.

I began to strum a rhythm on the open strings. I probably began to bounce my knee or tap my toe to emphasise the back beat. The still air in the kitchen began to be filled with sound, the quiet space seeming to come alive as the guitar's resonating body transferred its movements into the world around it. I began fingering melody lines and half-melodies, playing beneath the rhythm, exploring, guessing, discovering, *doing*. A descending melody line emerged and I repeated it immediately before it disappeared. Then I repeated and extended it, lost now in the world of sounds coming from the guitar.

But already there was too much. The six strings, ringing together beneath a melody line, seemed to fill up all the space, leaving no room for words or a vocal melody. I switched to a picking style, playing one or two strings at a time while retaining the same melody and rhythm. Now there was space in the sound – a gap big enough for some words to fit. But what words? I never know. The words I *think* of are never adequate, never sufficient. My 'thought words' never seem to me to reveal anything worth revealing. Instead, as usual, I focused on *playing*. I got lost in the sounds coming from the guitar. Perhaps it is the case that the music somehow 'distracts' me from what I am more consciously thinking about. Perhaps I move out of the cognitive realm into a more embodied world of physical movement and sound. Whatever, I was in that place now: not aware of trying to *think* anything at all, immersed in the moment and lost in the sounds. And then, a line came: 'Sometimes the good guy lucks out/And gets to live the dream'. Then other lines came too: 'Won't you stay close/Through your travels far afield/I've come to miss this thing/That feels so new to me'.

I knew the words were not independent of the events of the preceding weeks. I wasn't particularly trying to write about the situation in which Bradley and I found ourselves, yet I recognised the words as expressing in some way my feelings about – or my reaction to – *our* situation. I heard in the lyrics the sentiments of friends expressed in emails and phone calls. Brett had given me a lift and a more optimistic perspective when he had written, 'you're a great guy, and sometimes things go well for the good guy too'. Later, I guessed this was the 'source' of the line 'Sometimes the good guy lucks out/And gets to live the dream'. Likewise, the sentiments Deb expressed when she wrote, 'Sometimes things work out simply because they have to. You just have to stay open to the possibilities' perhaps related a sense of optimism when I found myself at a time – and a chord change – that felt like a chorus of sorts. To a chord change and melody that seemed to appear by magic, that I found irresistible, I sang:

> We will find a way
> We will find our way
> We will find that we …

It was at this point that the emerging narrative seemed to freeze. I didn't know where to go. There was simply nothing I felt able to sing here, no words I was willing to utter.

The story stopped and I was lost. Looking back, I think I was attempting to resolve our uncertain situation, to provide a comforting closure or resolution. But this comforting resolution was not something in which I believed. In my mind, I *could not* see how things would work out when Bradley moved to the US. I had no answers I imagined only endings. Yet I could not bring myself to utter, to re-inscribe in song, this troubling and painful outcome of separation, loss; the painful ending that was in the forefront of my mind. I didn't want these possible outcomes – in real life or in song.

Then something strange happened, something that, to me, demonstrates the once in a while profundity of songwriting. My singing literally stalled. I reached a point when I could not find words to continue the story of the song. Instead, I found myself repeating – once, twice, three times – with the music, the last word of the line, 'we', in place of a continuing narrative, to fill time almost. At some point during this repetition, the next line came and it was not a line I would have expected. After 'We will find that we, we, we…' the line that followed was simply: 'This time it's not just me'. The line came with an immediate sense of relief.

Perhaps, in searching for the next line (what was to come) I had become aware through the repetition of the previous line (what had gone before) that the defining word was not 'I' or 'me' but 'we'. Perhaps this simple line was enough to make me realise I did not have to be alone, that *we* could face the future *together*. I experienced this seemingly simple line as a kind of revelation. It brought light and a sense of hope. *I* had no answers to what would happen when Bradley left. Yet, I had stumbled upon some hope, some optimism, through the simple but profound realisation that this time, 'I' was a 'we'. *We* were in this together and it wasn't all down to *me*. For once it was *us*, it was *we*.

I sang the new song several times that day and I continue to sing it now Bradley has moved back to New York. I think it brought – and continues to bring – a different perspective on our situation, a perspective that I find more connected and hopeful than the one that tends to pervade my 'rational' or 'objective' thinking. It expresses my feelings and situation somehow more hopefully than I find myself able to do in words alone. I sent Bradley the song and, when he has needed words from me, I've wanted to ask him to listen again to the song: 'It's all in the song'.

Regardless of whether it is considered a 'good' song or not, writing and singing it has helped me discover – or, perhaps, helped me recreate – the meaning, significance and importance of a close personal relationship. Perhaps the song allows me to *show* a level of interpersonal connection and understanding that I would find impossible to *tell* in words alone. Perhaps the song has allowed me to tap into and express other areas of my being, other forms of knowing.

REFLECTIONS ON CONNECTIONS

Leonard Cohen has said, 'I don't know where the good songs come from or else I'd go there more often' (cited in Zollo, 2003, p. 345). I don't know either. But, after

20 years of trying to write songs, I do recognise some characteristics of the songwriting process, which I see inhabiting the preceding story. While these characteristics are hard to pin down – they are slippery, illusive and ambiguous – they are, I think, important in that they distinguish *writing* from *not writing*. Through reflecting on the story, I want now to highlight three key themes or strands that permeate my story of writing this particular song, and perhaps help distinguish writing from not writing. I see these strands as connecting with my experiences of writing other songs, with the stories of other songwriters, and (to a greater or lesser extent) with others' accounts of doing creative, arts-based or autoethnographic research.

Two qualifications, however, are needed. First, I do not wish to suggest that these three themes are the *only* issues of significance in the story. Stories are, ultimately, irreducible – no summary can do the work of the story – therefore further themes or strands inevitably lurk within the story. I accept that a degree of ambiguity and paradox (both inherent in the creative process itself and generated through the processes of storying) implies that precise 'conclusions' concerning the creative writing process are neither possible nor desirable. Thus, I hope readers will make their own interpretations and draw their own insights from the story, which may differ from what I discuss below. Second, Bob Dylan has said about songwriting, 'There's no rhyme or reason to it. There's no rule. That's what makes it so *attractive*' (cited in Zollo, 2003, p. 72). By trying to 'make sense' of songwriting I risk imposing 'artificial reason' on a process which may be devoid of reason. I highlight this possibility here not least because others may achieve creative successes through processes that differ markedly from those I describe.

Vulnerability

The first theme, which I think is strongly evident in the first part of the story, is a sense of what I can best describe as *vulnerability*. During this time a strong – overpowering even – sense of uncertainty, of 'un-knowing' is present as suggested in the line, 'All I had were questions. All I had were fears'. Reading the story again now, I gain a sense of my perceived inability to control, or even influence, the future path of an important personal relationship. One potentially significant consequence of this 'un-knowing' is that I asked questions: 'Would he return? Would I move with him? How could I make a life in a country in which I had no citizenship rights?' The importance of questioning, I think, becomes clear in the third section of the story, which focuses on writing the song. Here, the songwriting process might be seen as an effort to seek some kind of 'answer' to my questions. In the story, I experience finding – through writing – an 'answer' in the form of a personally meaningful perspective or orientation to questions which seem (to me) to have no obvious or logical resolution. In this sense, a degree of vulnerability may be significant because it stimulates questions that provide an incentive to write.

A sense of vulnerability recurs in the third section of the story in terms of my perception of a lack of 'control' of the songwriting process itself. In other words, I have the sense that to write a song I must be in a place which is, in some respect at least, unfamiliar or unresolved. Leonard Cohen suggests something similar in his description of what he must 'offer' the writing process. In his words:

> Well, things come so damn slow. Things come and they come and it's a tollgate, and they're particularly asking for something that you can't manage. They say, 'We got the goods here. What do you got to pay?' Well, I've got my intelligence, I've got a mind. 'No, we don't want that.' I've got my whole training as a poet. 'No, we don't want that.' I've got some licks, I've got some skills with my fingers on the guitar. 'No, we don't want that either.' Well, I've got a broken heart. 'No, we don't want that.' I've got a pretty girl-friend. 'No, we don't want that.' I've got sexual desire. 'No, we don't want that.' I've got a whole lot of things and the tollgate keeper says, 'That's not going to get it. We want you in a condition that you are not accustomed to. And that you yourself cannot name. We want you in a condition of receptivity that you cannot produce by yourself.' How are you going to come up with that? (cited in Zollo, 2003, p. 335)

I find this a revealing expression of what I too experience in songwriting; namely that when it comes to the next song, whatever you know, whatever you have, whatever you did *before*, is no longer enough. To write, Cohen seems to suggest, it is necessary to be 'some place new'. For me, this 'condition of receptivity' or 'condition that you are not accustomed to' is closely tied to vulnerability and uncertainty. It leads me to wonder about the extent to which resolution, knowing, certainty, and familiarity may be enemies of the creative process.

Discovery

Related to a sense of vulnerability and 'un-knowing', I think, is a second theme which sees songwriting as a process of *discovery*. A sense of discovery is evident in the third section of the story, for example in the lines, 'I began fingering melody lines and half-melodies, playing beneath the rhythm, exploring, guessing, discovering, *doing*. A descending melody line emerged and I repeated it immediately before it disap-peared'. This theme is also evident in Paul Simon's description of the songwriting process:

> You want your mind to wander, and to pick up words and phrases and fool with them and drop them. As soon as your mind knows that it's on and it's supposed to produce some lines, either it *doesn't* or it produces things that are very predictable. And that's why I say I'm not interested in writing something that I thought about. I'm interested in *discovering* where my mind wants to go, or what object it wants to pick up. It *always* picks up on something true. You'll find out much more about what you're thinking that way than you will if you're determined to say something. What you're determined to say is filled with all your rationalizations and your defenses and all of that. *What you want to say to the world* as opposed to what you're thinking. And as a *lyricist*, my job is to find out what it is that I'm thinking. Even if it's something that I don't want to be thinking. (cited in Zollo, 2003, pp. 97–8, emphasis in original)

I very much identify with this sense of 'discovering' stories through words and melodies as a way to 'find out what I am thinking' or 'pick up on something true'.
Jackson Browne describes similar experiences:

> It would be so much easier if you knew what you wanted to write about and where you wanted to arrive, but it just doesn't happen to work that way for me. It's more like an oracle. The things that come out of your subconscious are much more capable of conveying the truth of the situation than what you're consciously able to summon (cited in Gleason, 2008, p. 65)

A similar orientation is prevalent throughout the third section of my story: that the writing process was not planned or mapped from the outset, but unfolded as it went along. There is a sense, which is true to my experience, that it is only possible to 'discover' a song because I am *not* in full control of the writing process. In this regard, relinquishing some degree of control may well be a necessary step towards successful arts-based research (Douglas and Carless, 2008).

Inherent in both Simon's and Browne's accounts are the sense of, in some way, getting *beyond* conscious thoughts to find something 'true'. This perspective brings with it a host of ontological and epistemological questions that are outside the scope of this book. One question which *is* however highly relevant to its topic is *What might be done to facilitate this stepping beyond 'conscious' thought?* Leonard Cohen provides a general response to this question when he states,

> My immediate realm of thought is bureaucratic and like a traffic jam … So to penetrate this chattering and this meaningless debate that is occupying most of my attention, I have to come up with something that really speaks to my deepest interest (cited in Zollo, 2003, p. 332)

In this remark, Cohen suggests *something* is necessary to 'penetrate this chattering and this meaningless debate that is occupying most of my attention'. For me, as the third section of my story suggests, the 'thing' is often music. A sense of the way in which playing the guitar, playing music, provides a trigger for a new story is present, for example, in this excerpt:

> I focused on *playing*. I got lost in the sounds coming from the guitar. Perhaps it is the case that the music somehow 'distracts' me from what I am more consciously thinking about. Perhaps I move out of the cognitive realm into a more embodied world of physical movement and sound. Whatever, I was in that place now: not aware of trying to *think* anything at all, immersed in the moment and lost in the sounds. And then, a line came …

A sense of playing music leading to words is also present in this excerpt from an interview with the songwriter John Hiatt:

> *Do your songs always start with music?*
> Yeah, always. Maybe fifteen or twenty years ago, I might have had an axe to grind, or some brilliant insight that I was certain that you had to hear about. [Laughs] So I would

write that first. But now lyrics, really, are the last thing I do. And they take the most time.

Do you finish the whole melody before working on words?

No. Usually I'll get a chord pattern going, and that will evoke a melody, and I'll start singing nonsense. And then the nonsense will actually start to take shape into words (cited in Zollo, 2003, p. 646)

While a sense of 'discovering' meaning is also present in this excerpt, a key point for me is that it is the experience of *doing* – of playing music – which somehow permits or allows the words and stories to take shape.

Embodiment

The above accounts introduce what I consider to be a third theme or strand present in the story. This theme may be described as *embodiment*. More specifically, my story illustrates the way in which songwriting is ignited (and sustained) through an *embodied process*. A sense of an embodied process is evident, for example, in this excerpt from my story:

> From just one weighty strum, the six strings resonated through the back of the guitar and I could feel the movement of the wood against my stomach as I sat at the kitchen table … I began to strum a rhythm on the open strings. I probably began to bounce my knee or tap my toe to emphasise the back beat. The still air in the kitchen began to be filled with sound, the quiet space seeming to come alive as the guitar's resonating body transferred its movements into the world around it.

For me at least, it is this kind of 'embodied action' – as opposed to cognitive thought – that makes songwriting happen. It is the physical *doing-ness* that leads to music, stories, and words. In creative terms, as Blumenfeld-Jones (2002) puts it, 'understanding will only flow from your doing' (p. 90). In this regard, as Pelias (2008) notes, 'Unlike traditional scholarship where the body seems to slip away, performers generate and present their insights through the body, a knowing body, dependent on its participatory and empathic capacities' (p. 188). Through reliance on the body as an essential component in the creative process, songwriting appears to have much in common with arts-based, performative and autoethnographic inquiry.

Once creative writing is accepted as an embodied process, a host of biographical and material factors can be seen as potentially significant to the writing process. The second section of my story foregrounds the importance of these factors in the process of writing this particular song. One important presence is my guitar, which I portray as an object that holds personal meaning and significance as a result, in part at least, of biographical factors. John Hiatt describes the importance of the instrument in the following exchange:

> *Does the guitar you use affect the song?*
>
> Absolutely. There are songs inside guitars. For sure. The question is how you get them out of there.

And what's the answer?
For me, it's to sit down and start playing, because it's fun to play. If I'm lucky, something will hit me. If not, I keep playing (cited in Zollo, 2003, p. 647)

Besides reinforcing the way *playing* leads the creative process, this excerpt describes one view of why a *particular* instrument can be important to creativity: because certain guitars 'contain' songs!

In my story, I suggest that I formed some kind of 'relationship' with a particular instrument through finding and purchasing the guitar on my first trip to New York with Bradley, and through performing with the guitar at my grandmother's funeral. Through these processes, I see this guitar as coming to hold meaning for me as a result of 'our' history together. The result was, 'this instrument felt familiar and, somehow, it was comforting just sitting with it. This guitar already felt like a friend'. I think this point is significant in the context of an embodied creative songwriting process which necessarily involves the creation of *meaning*. Through an initial vulnerability leading to a need to question (and, accordingly, seek 'answers') combined with the opportunity of 'discovery' through writing, I see songwriting as a meaning-making process. To write a meaningful song, I very often need personally meaningful 'props'. A prop – namely, in this instance, a guitar – is thus more than an essential tool; it can also be an effective way to bring embodied meaning to the creative enterprise.

LETTING GO

After writing over 6000 words about writing songs, have I raised more questions than I have answered? *Is* the songwriting process relevant to writing autoethnographic texts? *Does* my story show creative processes in action in a way that might be useful to others? By selecting three characteristics of *my* writing process (vulnerability, discovery and embodiment) have I done 'symbolic violence' to the diversity and possibility of others' creative processes? Should I have written about – and published – details of *my* personal life which reveal aspects of *others'* lives?

These are tough questions to answer, but are exactly the kinds of questions faced by those who choose to use autoethnography in their research. By giving their consent to be included in my story, Bradley, Brett, Deb, Julie and Kitrina may have cleared my 'ethical conscience'. Yet I remain unsure if I've done the 'right thing'. I just got off the phone to Bradley and during the call I asked him how vulnerability, discovery and embodiment fitted *his* experience of creativity through dance. His response was supportive but he felt that there were many other potentially important strands too. For him, for example, a creative process might stem from even the shortest line or quote from a story or a song. It is clear that the picture I have offered is a partial one: it is far from complete. It is also strongly situated in my own experience. Perhaps, in this light, the chapter is best considered as a series of questions rather than answers? Perhaps asking the 'right' questions is enough?

Perhaps it is time to let go …

Summary

- Some of the best experiences emerge from synchronicities that need to be noticed and acted on.
- Songwriting is a form of lyric inquiry and can also bring understanding and insight.
- Letting go of the creation is an important part of the process.
- Good ideas emerge when you are not trying hard to compose.
- Songs can show a level of interpersonal connection that is impossible to tell in words alone.
- Vulnerability should be acknowledged, and a period of 'unknowing' recognised as the precursor or discovering of ideas.
- Songwriting is an embodied action.

Acknowledgments

I want to thank Bradley, Brett, Deb, Julie and Kitrina for allowing me to write them into the story I have presented here. I also thank Kitrina Douglas, Tessa Muncey and Bradley Shelver for generously sharing with me their insights into autoethnography, narrative research and the creative process – their inputs have helped to shape the chapter. Finally, I thank Paul Zollo and Da Capo Press for kindly granting permission to quote from the interviews Paul Zollo conducted in his book *Songwriters on Songwriting* (expanded edition).

REFERENCES

Blumenfeld-Jones, D. (2002) If I Could Have Said it, I Would Have. In C. Bagley and M. Cancienne (Eds) *Dancing the Data*. Peter Lang, New York, pp. 90–104.

Chase, S. (2005) Narrative Inquiry: Multiple lenses, approaches, voices. In N. Denzin and Y. Lincoln (Eds) *Handbook of Qualitative Research* (3rd edn). Sage, Thousand Oaks, CA, pp 651–79.

Cole, A. and Knowles, J. (2008) Arts-informed Research. In J. Knowles and A. Cole (Eds) *Handbook of the Arts in Qualitative Research*. Sage, Thousand Oaks, CA, pp. 55–70.

Douglas, K. and Carless, D. (2005) *Across the Tamar: Stories from women in Cornwall*. Audio CD.

Douglas, K. and Carless, D. (2008) Nurturing a performative self. *Forum Qualitative Sozialforschung* [Forum: Qualitative Social Research], **9**(2), Art. 23. Retrieved October 2008, from http://www.qualitative-research.net/fqs-texte/2-08/08-2-23-e.htm

Gleason, H. (2008) Jackson Browne: Summoning a sky blue and black. *American Songwriter*, **23**(6), 58–67.

Holman Jones, S. (2005) Autoethnography: Making the personal political. In N. Denzin and Y. Lincoln (Eds) *Handbook of Qualitative Research* (3rd edn). Sage, Thousand Oaks, CA, pp. 763–97.

Lennon, J. and McCartney, P. (1968). 'Julia', from the *White Album*. Apple, London.

Lewis, P. (2006) Stories I teach–live by. *Qualitative Inquiry*, **12**(5), 829–49.

Neilsen, L. (2008) Lyric Inquiry. In J. Knowles and A. Cole (Eds) *Handbook of the Arts in Qualitative Research*. Sage, Thousand Oaks, CA, pp. 93–102.

Pelias, R. (2008) Performative Inquiry: Embodiment and its challenges. In J. Knowles and A. Cole (Eds) *Handbook of the Arts in Qualitative Research*. Sage, Thousand Oaks, CA, pp. 185–93.

Zollo, P. (2003) *Songwriters on Songwriting* (exp. edn). Da Capo Press, Cincinnati, OH.

POSTSCRIPT

At the end of Jane Eyre there is an unequivocal conclusion to the relationship of Jane and Mr Rochester when she states 'Reader, I married him' (Brontë, 1966 [1847], p. 474). John Fowles (1981) gives us slightly more choice of how things turn out in *The French Lieutenant's Woman*, with two possible endings to the story. The first of Fowles' two endings is the 'happy' one where a child is the healer of the breach between Charles and Sarah. In the second ending, Fowles appears and turns back the clock so we can see what might/did/should have happened. This time there is no understanding, nor is there any love left between Charles and Sarah. We are led to assume that Sarah was only a deceiver after all and that they part.

At the end of my story there is no unequivocal conclusion, nor is there an opportunity to turn back the clock. Like all autoethnographies, this text is partial and fragmentary. It is devised from my own experience of performing my own story and from the reactions to that story, via the synchronicities that have introduced me to philosophers, novelists, poets, playwrights, songwriters and much more. Once something is known it cannot be unknown. Having come to the end of the book, both the newcomer and the experienced may have many questions, comments and criticisms, but at the end I am reminded of the words of a very wise woman, Ann Walton, who was among many things, my mentor, my counsellor, my supervisor and my spiritual guide, and without whom none of my story would ever have been told.

One day she was telling me that she was going to talk to a group of people about Polarity Theory (Sills, 1989). Now this is a brave theory that attempts to combine western and eastern thought into a truly holistic approach to understanding the body. I arrived at it with a sympathy for new-age thinking but realise it is not for faint-hearted sceptics, which was what I thought this group might consist of. 'Aren't you afraid they will think you are mad?' I asked her. After a slight pause she looked at me, smiled and said, 'Tessa, you can only be responsible for what you say, not how it is received'. This, I realise, has stood me in good stead as I recoil from the verbal and textual responses to what I have said or written. You, the reader, are responsible for your interpretation of my ideas; the onus is on you to follow up the trails of references I have left, or not. We have engaged in a brief meeting of minds and I hope the outcome may echo the sentiments of Zeldin (1998, p. 14), who says 'Conversation is a meeting of minds with different memories and habits.

When minds meet, they don't just exchange facts; they transform them, reshape them, draw different implications from them, engage in new trains of thought'. I look forward to these new conversations.

Summary

In short, an autoethnography consists of:

- identification of a meaningful experience that you are prepared to share
- an engagement in an iterative relationship between your research and your personal experiences
- a selection of creative means to transform the experience
- showing, not telling
- an expectation of criticism and the ammunition needed to counter it
- recognition of the role of synchronicities in steering the development of your work
- immense satisfaction from the personal growth that ensues.

REFERENCES

Brontë, C. (1966 [1847]) *Jane Eyre*. Penguin, Harmondsworth.
Fowles, J. (1981) *The French Lieutenant's Woman*. New American Library, New York.
Sills, F. (1989) *The Polarity Process*. Element Books, Shaftesbury.
Zeldin, T. (1998) *Conversation: How talk can change your life*. Harvill Press, London.

INDEX